W9-BMO-670

SARAH ZACHARIAS DAVIS

author of *Transparent*

The Friends We Keep

Discussion Guide Inside

A Woman's Quest
for the Soul *of* Friendship

Praise for
The Friends We Keep

"Friendships take years to cultivate yet can be lost in a matter of minutes. Sarah Zacharias Davis deftly explores the complex terrain of that human bond, explaining why so many of us long to be known and how important it is cultivate at least a few faithful people who will stand beside us the rest of our lives."

—JULIA DUIN, religion editor for the *Washington Times* and author of *Quitting Church: Why the Faithful Are Fleeing and What to Do About It*

"Sarah's words could not come at a better time. Too many of us have allowed our female friendships to slip on the priority scale, and this book is the perfect reminder of the essential, beautifully ordained connection between women. Reading and relishing her words, I recalled with rich nostalgia the formative friendships of my childhood and emerged from the pages with a fresh perspective and heightened appreciation for the special women in my life today. This book reads like the voice of a friend, intimate and true."

—KRISTIN ARMSTRONG, contributing editor for *Runner's World* magazine and author of four books, including *Happily Ever After: Walking with Peace and Courage Through a Year of Divorce* and *Work in Progress: An Unfinished Woman's Guide to Grace*

"*The Friends We Keep* is a true and tender testimony to the joys and struggles we women experience in our friendships with one another. As I read I found myself nodding in agreement and sometimes tearing up in remembrance. We don't always get it right, but we need each other—and there is deep satisfaction to be found in the relationships we forge. I loved Sarah's book and recommend it to anyone who seeks to know (or find) her truest friends."

—LEIGH MCLEROY, author of *The Beautiful Ache* and *Treasured*

The Friends We Keep

The Friends We Keep

A Woman's *Quest*
for the *Soul* of Friendship

SARAH
ZACHARIAS DAVIS

WaterBrook
PRESS

THE FRIENDS WE KEEP
PUBLISHED BY WATERBROOK PRESS
12265 Oracle Boulevard, Suite 200
Colorado Springs, Colorado 80921

Scripture quotations are taken from the Holy Bible, New International Version®.
NIV®. Copyright © 1973, 1978, 1984 by International Bible Society. Used by
permission of Zondervan Publishing House. All rights reserved.

ISBN 978-1-4000-7439-6
ISBN 978-0-307-44611-4 (electronic)

Published in the United States by WaterBrook Multnomah, an imprint of the Crown
Publishing Group, a division of Random House Inc., New York.

WATERBROOK and its deer colophon are registered trademarks of Random House Inc.

Library of Congress Cataloging-in-Publication Data
Davis, Sarah Zacharias, 1975–
    The friends we keep : a woman's quest for the soul of friendship / Sarah Zacharias
Davis. — 1st ed.
        p. cm.
    Includes bibliographical references.
    ISBN 978-1-4000-7439-6 — ISBN 978-0-307-44611-4 (electronic)
    1. Christian women—Religious life. 2. Female friendship—Religious aspects—
Christianity. I. Title.
    BV4527.D385 2009
    241'.6762—dc22

                                        2009004171

Printed in the United States of America
2009—First Edition

10 9 8 7 6 5 4 3 2 1

SPECIAL SALES
Most WaterBrook Multnomah books are available at special quantity discounts when
purchased in bulk by corporations, organizations, and special-interest groups. Custom
imprinting or excerpting can also be done to fit special needs. For information, please
e-mail SpecialMarkets@WaterBrookMultnomah.com or call 1-800-603-7051.

For my friends:
You enrich my life immeasurably.

I awoke this morning with a devout thanksgiving for my friends, the old and the new.

RALPH WALDO EMERSON

Contents

ONE

Whom Do You Call Friend?

My eyes flooded with tears that began rolling down my face. Horrified at my public display of grief, I had to keep myself from all-out sobbing over Isabel's death before the person sitting next to me on the plane thought me mentally unstable and requested to be moved to another seat.

This was my third time reading the book *The Saving Graces*, and I cried all three times when each of the friends read Isabel's letters after her death. I stumbled upon *The Saving Graces*, a novel by Patricia Gaffney, one evening when perusing Barnes and Noble for something good. The words "*New York Times* Bestseller" caught my eye, and I decided to give Gaffney a try, though I was unfamiliar with anything she had written.

The Saving Graces is the story of four friends and how each is there for the others through the ups and downs of life: childlessness, broken relationships, love, illness, and death. I read the book three times because I wanted to join the friendship circle of Lee, Rudy, Isabel, and Emma again and because it deeply impacted the way I viewed friendship, both the kind of friendships I wanted and the kind of friend I wanted to be. For me *The Saving Graces* raised the bar, as well as the stakes. I loved the way the others supported Rudy when she moved out of her home and through the abuse she encountered. The unmitigated appreciation for each individual friend was evidenced as Isabel wrote parting letters to her three friends. I was inspired by the manner with which the friends got snippy with each other and yet quickly forgave and forgot.

Finally, I was moved by how the loss of one left an enormous hole that could not, nor would, ever be filled in the others. I found this especially, exquisitely stunning, thus moving me to tears each time I shared these women's lives. They were there to defend, laugh, comfort, give physical care, and even give space—all that real life requires. These were friendships of depth and honesty, strength and longevity. These friends loved each other in all their messiness. No one had to bring perfection to the friendship, only loyalty.

My reluctance to leave the world of the four women and close the book for the third time invited explorational thoughts of friendship. What was it about their friendships that left me reluctant to leave their company and return to my own life? Is that what my friendships were supposed to look like? Did I need to find a Rudy, an Isabel, a Lee, or an Emma to fill the longing that this novel surreptitiously uncovered in my soul? Did my own small collection of friendships seem not enough compared to the bond these four shared? And why not? Was it the way they supported one another or the way they always made time for one another? Or was it the way one could behave in a manner that was very unlovable and yet still remain loved?

At the risk of making a grand, sweeping gender statement, I'll point out that some men seem to have categories of friends. They have work friends, friends for playing weekly pickup basketball games, golfing friends, and friends forced on them by a significant other. Seldom do they see these friends outside their category of identity, yet they would call them friends. Many of the friendships women hold, however, seem to make their way beyond the circumstances that brought them together and meander into their lives through both the valleys and the peaks, eventually ending up in the women's souls, where they can both restore and destruct. And yet, isn't a real friendship one that would bring both the yin and the yang, so to speak? Is the multidimensional aspect of the relationship the very characteristic that makes it a true friendship? Would I have been so captivated and, yes, envious of the saving graces if their friendships contained no shadows?

History is rife with story upon story of love, commitment, bravery, loyalty, betrayal, and disappointment—all within friendships. And in our own personal histories, many of the same stories can be told. Friendship is a relationship we desire and cultivate early in our development, whether we had an imaginary friend as a constant companion or we began the first day of school as shy, pigtailed little girls inviting another to be our friend.

For a woman, the connection to friendship is innate and essential. It feels so vital to living that the desire for it seems part of our fabric of being. Cicero said friendship "springs from nature rather than from need—from an inclination of the mind with a certain consciousness of love."[1] This is certainly true across generations and cultures.

Early Chinese culture held women's friendships as almost sacred. In her beautiful work of historical fiction *Snow Flower and the Secret Fan,* Lisa See educates her readers about sacred friendship practices.[2] The Chinese women of this patriarchal culture committed themselves to very deep friendships, knowing there was substance and soul that could exist in no other relationships.

There were two types of soul friendships: sworn sisters and *laotong,* which means "old same." Sworn sisterhoods were groups of unmarried women who became friends. These sisterhoods dissolved at the time of marriage. A laotong relationship was between two girls from different villages. Many superstitions were observed before two girls would be found to be a match. They were usually the same age and both born in auspicious years, according to the tradition.

The girls were bound together in lifelong friendship, in a ceremony that was nearly equivalent to a marriage ceremony in its commitments and gravity. The larger world only learned of the existence of this tradition of special friendships when, in a crowded train station at the height of China's Cultural Revolution, a woman was detained as a suspected spy after fainting. Authorities searched her belongings in an effort to identify her and found papers written in a language none could identify. Scholars were brought in to examine the writings, and they discovered that the elderly woman was not a spy after all; rather, her writings were in a secret language used only by Yao women in South China. This language had been a secret for more than a thousand years.

Sadly, most of the writings in *nu shu* have not survived over the years as they were either buried with the women at their death to accompany them to the other world or destroyed in the revolution. In the twentieth century, the nu shu language is all but extinct and no longer needed. But its existence and use discloses the depth of friendship and community among these women—and the universal, powerful longing for friendship that exists among us, the desire to be known and heard.

How do you know your friends, and how do you find

them? Most of us look back on lives decorated with stories of friendships from the time we were young.

There are the friends we hurried home from school to play with every day. After donning playclothes and perhaps wolfing down a snack, we'd join them for some clandestine adventure until we were summoned to dinner at dusk.

There are the friends who gave us our social life when we were teenagers, inviting us to something somewhere that opened an entire new world of cliques, jealousy, loyalty, and, ultimately, resiliency.

There are the friends of our early twenties, alongside whom we entered independence, straddling worlds of co-dependency and experimental autonomy.

There are the friends who champion us through many of the celebrations of adult life, from marriage and professional promotions to buying a first home and having children, along with the disappointments and a myriad of heartbreaks and losses.

And there's every kind of friend in between: the friend you go to the ballet with; the friend you shop with—the one who talks you into a regrettable purchase every time; the one who will tell you what you want to hear and the one who has the courage to tell you what you don't; the friend from whom you always get the latest news on everyone else; the one who will listen when you need to be heard and the one who will talk when you only have energy to listen. There's the role model, the mentor, and the friend with whom you have a love-hate relationship. There are group and work friendships, friendships within a larger community, the "our children are best friends" and "our husbands are best friends" relationships.

If so many different types of connections are called friendships, do they all come from the same well, some single essence of friendship? What is it that creates a friendship? Is it social obligation, the fact that you wanted a large wedding party so the pictures would look better, necessity, or essential longing? And if it is longing, is the primary catalyst our longing for someone's friendship or that person's longing for ours? Do we need to know the answers to these questions to be a good friend or to have a fulfilling friendship—or am I simply overanalyzing that which just happens naturally?

My worn paperback copy of *The Saving Graces* placed back on my shelf of fiction between authors Fielding and Grisham, these were the questions I went looking to answer.

For centuries poets, authors, songwriters, and screenplay writers have sought to define friendship—with results ranging from Aristotle's conclusion that friendship is "a single soul dwelling in two bodies" to Ralph Waldo Emerson's description of a friend as "a person with whom I may be sincere."[3]

Certainly a distinction should be made between an acquaintance and a true friend. Is friendship simply companionship? For me, this is not the case. *The Saving Graces* taught me a narrower, even sacred definition of friendship.

What qualifies someone to be called your friend?

I read a sweet story by F. W. Boreham about a little boy plagued by nightmares.[4] Rather than visions of sugarplums, a frightening tiger intrudes on the boy's dreams. Night after night the child wakes in fear, in a cold sweat, and with a rapidly beating heart. His parents are concerned (and probably lacking sleep if the boy is crawling into bed with them each night), and they send him to a child psychologist.

After listening to the boy recount his dreams, the psychologist gets an idea. He tells the child, "The tiger visiting you is actually a good tiger. He wants to be your friend. So next time the tiger appears in your dream, simply put your hand out to shake his paw and say, 'Hello, old chap!'"

And so, the story goes, that very same night the boy asleep in his bed suddenly becomes restless. He thrashes about, sweating and crying out in his sleep, until a small hand, partly hidden by cotton pajamas, suddenly juts out from the covers, followed by a sleepy little voice saying, "Hello, old chap!" Thus he made friends with the tiger.

That story makes me smile, and I suppose this is partly because of the old English language that scripts a little boy using amusing terms like "old chap." But is that how it's done? Is mere familiarity how friendships are forged? Does simply banishing the title of stranger make way for friendship? Or is something more required?

Perhaps it is the banishing of danger. The reason the tiger

trick worked on the little boy's nightmares was that it removed the danger. Maybe that works in making friends too. Maybe beyond simple introductions so that we are no longer strangers, we enter a shared space with a person who we hope is safe—safe for us to be ourselves and to be real.

What creates that safe space? Is it simply shared interests or geography? Is friendship born in similar goals or experiences? What about behavior? If two people act in a certain way toward each other, are they friends? If so, then what does friendship look like?

As I thought about how art imitates life, and ever a lover of art—paintings, literature, poetry, films, and music—I mulled the characteristics of friendship and the numerous recent pictures of friendship, specifically women's friendships. When I interact with these different media, something in them resonates with me, something that moves me, and I stop and notice. Whether it's a tearjerker movie, a painting whose brush strokes create a gentle gesture, or lyrics so poignant, art inspires me to pay attention to what is within myself.

In the 1980s film *The Four Seasons,* the opening scene depicts three couples going away for a few days in the spring. Toasts and speeches characterize this holiday together, and the couples celebrate the depth of their friendships. We learn that the men were introduced to each other after the women became friends. The following season, summer, one friend is missing. During the previous few months, one couple has divorced and a cute young girlfriend has joined the circle to now complete the six.

I couldn't help but wonder what happened to the wife. Why is she eliminated from the circle of friends? And if the women were the original friends, why have they agreed to oust her from the group? Why doesn't the divorced couple at least get joint custody of their friends?

Throughout the movie's four seasons, we see what each friend brings to the circle of friendship. We see the idiosyncrasies, bad habits, and selfishness but also the commitment to one another through all the terrain in each season of friendship. And when one woman cries out in sheer frustration that, in spite of it all, she needs her friends and always will, we feel the truth of her statement reverberate through us. This was a climactic exclamation after months of tension created by selfishness, lack of awareness, and judgment between the friends. But, yes, in spite of the hurts our friendships can cause, we need them, we want them.

Growing up, I adored reading and seeing films of *Anne of Green Gables.* I still do. Anne, an imaginative and precocious orphan, comes to live with an aging pair of siblings, neither of whom has ever married. Marilla, a salty, no-nonsense woman, doesn't have either the understanding or the patience for Anne's emotions and antics. Matthew, her brother, is a soft-spoken and kindhearted man, though timid too. When Anne arrives in Avonlea and is invited to become part of

Matthew and Marilla Cuthbert's family, she sets out to make a friend. But Anne isn't looking for just any acquaintance; rather, she is in search of a "kindred spirit," a "bosom friend."

"A—a what kind of a friend?" Marilla asked her, puzzled.

"A bosom friend—an intimate friend, you know—," Anne replied, "a really kindred spirit to whom I can confide my inmost soul. I've dreamed of meeting her all my life. I never really supposed I would, but so many of my loveliest dreams have come true all at once that perhaps this one will, too. Do you think it's possible?"

Later, after learning more about a potential bosom friend, Anne adds one more requirement: "Oh, I'm so glad she's pretty. Next to being beautiful oneself—and that's impossible in my case—it would be best to have a beautiful bosom friend."[5]

With the unflinching honesty of a child, Anne expresses what we all secretly desire: a best, kindred-spirit kind of friend. The older we get, the more reluctant we are to ask for what we want or need, but Anne does so unabashedly. And in her eyes, her friendship with Diana is made even better when her new friend is someone that Anne herself is convinced she could never be. Could it be that we go in search of friends who embody something we wish we were or long to be?

The Big Chill, noted for the new ground it forged as both the first film with an ensemble cast of more than one known actor and one of the earliest to use popular music rather than original scores, explored the best-of-friends idea. The movie, treasured in part for its well-loved soundtrack and its famous football and kitchen cleanup dance scenes, brings seven old school friends together after the eighth member of their group passes away. The friends have fallen mostly out of touch with one another, and together they relive old days in the glow of nostalgia that often lights the picture differently than we saw events at the time. They speak of regrets both past and present, and as the friends get reacquainted, they become agents of change in one another's lives.

In one of the film's most surprising scenes, Sarah, a character played by Glenn Close, in an act of both personal redemption for past wrongs and true, unselfish friendship, makes a startling decision of sacrificial love for her friend Meg. Even with the personal implications that belie altruistic motives, the act is so magnanimous it seems quite unreal.

But that is what we want from our friends, isn't it, though we seldom dare to hope or ask—those who will do anything for us, committing acts that can save our lives from falling apart or at least hold our dreams intact?

The well-known friendship film *Beaches* beckons us to follow the journey of a friendship between two entirely dissimilar women whom we first glimpse as little girls. Though they couldn't be more different in appearance, upbringing, or personality, the girls are drawn instantly to each other. We join them again as impressionable twenty-somethings trying on their dreams for size and seeing how they fit. As adults, they resign themselves to life, trying still to hold on to their dreams and find happiness amidst it all. They support each other, stab each other in the back, fight with each other, take turns snubbing each other, and ultimately need each other as a hot-tempered, red-headed CC Bloom stands by her pillow-lipped friend Hillary in the final days of Hillary's life—a life snuffed out much too soon, leaving behind a precocious little girl.

If you've seen the film, you know that watching the movie requires a box of tissues and introduced the well-known song "Wind Beneath My Wings." Sung by Bette Midler, who portrays the adult CC, the song became the solo staple at graduations, weddings, and long-distance dedications over the airwaves of schmaltzy late-night radio programs.

But there's a reason schmaltz resonates with us, even if we're too cool to admit it. We want to know that a true friendship can survive the years, the growing pains, and the inevitable changes we morph through and that in the end it will become triumphantly stronger than ever. When we see glimpses of this kind of friendship, we are touched, changed even. We want to know we will still be loved even when we have behaved badly, and we want reassurance that, for all the messiness over things so inconsequential, when it counts, all will be right again.

The enormously popular book *The Joy Luck Club* by

Amy Tan, which later became a movie, captures readers with its beautiful story of a group of women from China. For almost forty years the women meet to play mah-jongg. They eat, talk about their children, and most of all share their lives together—lives that are little known or understood by their daughters. Yet they share deep understanding. After forty years these women are truly known.

Fried Green Tomatoes gently brings us from present to past and then back to present again as an elderly lady in a nursing home befriends a lonely and defeated woman and tells her the powerful story of two unlikely friends bound together first by love, then by tragedy, and ultimately by vivacity. As we drift in and out of the story of this unique friendship, we, along with Kathy Bates's character, Evelyn Couch, are inspired by the depth of their friendship and the edges to which it will take them. Here in a friendship most unlikely, strength always protects vulnerability and gentleness soothes defiance.

Divine Secrets of the Ya-Ya Sisterhood, another book-to-movie story, depicts a powerful friendship among strong southern women. With fierce loyalty the friends bolster one another through bitter heartaches. The story celebrates life's resilience, if slightly deflated buoyancy, and the unconditional and sometimes tough love of friendship.

Why does each of these stories of friendship resonate so deeply, moving us to tears, contemplation, even imitation? Is it

the longevity, the gentle strength of having someone unflinch-
ingly on your side, another's strength to borrow when yours is
depleted, and the quest for love in spite of our shortcomings?

As we peer into the lives of these iconic friends, do they serve
as mirrors that accurately reflect our own experience? Women's
friendships often are portrayed as serendipitous relationships
characterized by conflict, jealousy, competitiveness, betrayal,
and disappointment—but ultimately demonstrating loyalty,
availability, kindred spirits, forgiveness, and fierce strength.
They are a little bit nurturance, a little bit group therapy.
There is perseverance, trust, protection, and faith.

Sounds like love, doesn't it? It is. Friendship in its truest,
purest form is love.

But what do we mean by love? I love chocolate, I love my
sister, and God loves me. Are those the same kind of love?
Does the word *love* used three times have the same meaning,
the same intensity, and demand the same actions and proofs?

Of course it doesn't, and so the Greeks used different
words—*agape, eros, philia*—to express different types of love.
Just as agape is a universal love and eros a passionate love and
sexual love, philia or brotherly love is the love of friendship.

C. S. Lewis maintains that friendship love is possibly the

least biological of the loves. While agape is of God and eros is innate within the fiber of our being, both a community and an individual can exist without friendship, Lewis says.[6]

But can it? Is friendship vital to our survival as individuals?

I suppose, in a sense, no. What sustains life is air and nutrition. And if we are looking for mere sustenance, then friendship is not vital to that. But most of us need friendship. We want more than mere sustenance. We're looking for people, experiences, and relationships that enrich our lives. Without friendships, who would join our heart in its many joys, its brokenness, its fears, its stillness, and its hopes? We are looking to feel deeper, love deeper, and ultimately live deeper, and so we seek friendship, sometimes in safe places and often in unexpected ones too.

In the pages ahead are explorations of the many facets of our friendships: How do we love? How do we hurt and bring pain to others? How do we bear another's burdens? And what texture do friendships bring to our lives? What about the friend who got away? What do we demand of our friendships? And more important, what do friendships require of us?

As I ponder these questions, I draw on multiple stories of real-life friendships, many directly from my own experience and others shared with me by women who are honestly wrestling through these same thorny issues. I've chosen not to identify the sources but have simply let each woman describe her experience to lead us deeper in thinking about the complexities of authentic intimacy.

But above all else this book is an exploration of the essence of friendship: after the twists and turns through the shadows and the light, what ultimately matters concerning friendship is that it is a gift.

> Friendship is not a reward for our discrimination and good taste in finding one another out. It is the instrument by which God reveals to each the beauties of all the others. They are no greater than the beauties of a thousand other men; by Friendship God opens our eyes to them. They are, like all beauties, derived from Him, and then, in a good Friendship, increased by Him through the Friendship itself, so that it is His instrument for creating as well as for revealing.[7]

TWO

The Roles We Play

"To forge connection, to create community, and to organize and orchestrate a girl's world so that she's at the center of it"[1]—these are the goals dictated by a little girl's brain, according to Louann Brizendine, neuropsychiatrist and author of *The Female Brain*.

Connection, community, organization of our worlds— what are the roles we play to do just that, and what are the roles that get in the way of what we are really searching for?

Let's take a look at some of the common friend roles today.

THE MEG FRIEND

"What in the world are you going to do now, Jo?" asked Meg one snowy afternoon, as her sister came tramping through the hall, in rubber boots, old sack, and hood, with a broom in one hand and a shovel in the other.

"Going out for exercise," answered Jo with a mischievous twinkle in her eyes.

"I should think two long walks this morning would have been enough! It's cold and dull out, and I advise you to stay warm and dry by the fire, as I do," said Meg with a shiver.[2]

Little Women is, of course, the classic and touching work by Louisa May Alcott that centers on the friendship of four sisters. The youngest is Amy, the curly-haired baby of the family. Beth is quiet, gentle, and sweet. Jo is loud and impetuous but has an enormous heart. She was played by Katharine Hepburn so perfectly in the original movie that to me Katharine Hepburn is Jo March. And then Meg, the oldest, is the nurturer, the mother, though the four girls already had a mother.

In friendships, as in most relationships, there are roles we take on and there are roles we fall into. What about the mothering role?

A Navajo tale tells of how a woman, First Woman, nurtured people from one world to another, caring for them and teaching them how to live. As the story goes, it was a time when humans were hardly dissimilar from animals, insects, and birds. They lived in the third world, and gradually, as distinctions between the species developed and they became more diverse, humans began to look more human, much as they do now.

As time went on and generations passed, there came a shortage of food and life-giving sustenance in the third world. People began to steal from one another as a means of survival because there was not enough to go around. Though they tried to plant and harvest food, they found no success.

The people decided that they should leave the world they knew and go in search of another world to inhabit. And so they flew away, seeking a new home because, though some were human, all the species could fly. They flew and flew, and still they found nothing.

Finally discouraged and defeated, they were ready to give up, which surely would have meant their demise. And then they heard voices calling to them. It was First Woman and her family. The people followed the voices and discovered a new world, the fourth world, filled with mountains and sky, rivers and rolling hills, and vast fields.

First Woman taught them how to bathe; how to grow and prepare food; how to wear moccasins, leggings, and other clothing; and how to fix their hair, rolled into double loops and tied at the backs of their heads. She advised them to earn the seed to plant their fields and thus sustain themselves. But some didn't want to bother with planting. They were content enough with seeds and berries they could gather in the forests. And others agreed they should plant their own fields but were loath to take the time to earn the seed. So instead the people sent groups in four different directions to steal corn from the Pueblos, who were already established in the fourth world.

As the groups returned from their misguided mission, they found that the cornstalks they lugged back with them were moldy or infested with bugs and rotted. Now they had no food and no plan. So they called a meeting, as communities of people are prone to do, and they invited First Woman. This time she advised them to send four women in four directions with gifts they could exchange for seed corn. The women went, and on their mission they also learned how to plant, how to grow, and how to harvest. The mission was a resounding success! The women returned with not only seed but also beans, squash, tobacco, and other herbs.

In time the fields stretched as far toward the horizon as eyes could see, and every year the four women who went out were honored. The women stored the seed during winter, and the women planted the seed (don't worry; the men had to prepare the fields). And as legend tells it, First Woman was forever known as their wise protector.[3]

This story confirms how we women have within us a nurturing instinct that crosses cultures, time, even species, that we see evidenced through story, tradition, and practice. That women possess a nurturing quality may seem like an archaic gender cliché today, but it is supported in studies done of collected research and in psychology as well.

After conducting studies of girls and boys at ages eight and eleven, psychologist Carol Gilligan sustains this idea in her book *In a Different Voice*. To eleven-year-old Jake and Amy, Gilligan posed these kinds of questions, at a child's level: "How would you describe yourself to yourself?" and, "If you had to describe the person you are in a way that you yourself would know it was you, what would you say?" and, "When responsibilities to oneself and to others conflict, how should you choose?"

Amy answered each question in the context of relationship to others. The author concludes, "To Jake's ideal of perfection, against which he measures the worth of himself, Amy counterposes an ideal of care, against which she measures the worth of her activity."[4]

There are women who embrace this role of nurturer, and by their admission they are born to be mothers. They nurture everything from their pets to their significant others. But for other women, this role is less natural. Though even for such a woman, if she was to become pregnant, the mothering instinct would emerge as her brain was stimulated by shifting levels of hormones.

But does nurturing and mothering become a role we play in friendships and not simply an action? When a friend nurtures, does she become more needed? Does she become the protector, the organizer, the caretaker? Is it a friend's role to make sure a friend eats right, gets enough rest, and feels good?

Certainly, the nurturing, mothering friend comes to the rescue when someone becomes confrontational. She organizes the outings, making sure reservations are made and everyone has directions. And when the evening is complete, she makes sure everyone gets home safely. She is always the one talking her friends down from the ledge. She is the first one called in a crisis. This is her role, and it makes her feel good—that she is a good person and a good friend. But these relationships often develop a codependency. And while interdependence is community, codependence is something quite different. Codependence allows a person to drain strength from us and gives us the opportunity to deplete strength from the other too, as we enable the codependency.

This nurturing, mothering kind of friendship is not sharing strength or even borrowing it for a while, as we all need to do from time to time. Rather this kind of friendship is giving, and it is giving without receiving anything in return. Then something else probably happens too. In relationships where one gives and one takes rather than both give *and* take, this nurturing friend finds there is no one to mother her. Where does she turn when she has an inevitable crisis or wants to have a meltdown? Where can she go when she needs someone to speak real wisdom into her life?

The nurturing, mothering friend probably won't go to the friends she mothers—and they may not handle it well if she does. When she just needs to fall, who is both prepared and strong enough to catch her? Her friends may see her as the strong one, the one who has it all together, not the one who is needy and confused, even on rare occasions. They may not be open to her having questions or seeming weak.

And perhaps we know this, and that is how we like it. Perhaps sometimes we are most comfortable in relationships where we are caring for others and are needed, rather than in relationships where we see ourselves as an equal, where there is give and take, where we could potentially feel indebted to another, and where someone could actually be better than we are at being a friend. At least that is our fear. We fear the equalizing in a friendship would create an inevitable imbalance with us on the lighter end if she gives more than we do. This conscious scorekeeping could be a breeding ground for jealousy or accumulation of debt.

So then is it your pattern to give yourself fully to friendships where you can be the rescuer, be needed, be the nurturer and protector, and then hold back in friendships where you are less likely to play that role? Do we all need to be needed? And do we need to have more points on the giving board to feel secure? But we discover that living free of friendship debt does not afford freedom after all. Instead, if you earn love and you earn friendship with things you do, then you can just as easily unearn love or friendship if you cease to do those things.

That is what we each fear, isn't it?

THE EVIL QUEEN FRIEND
(The Second Fairest of Them All)

Everyone's had a friendship disrupted by jealousy. Whether we're on the receiving end or the feelings are ours to own, each of us can tell stories of jealousy in our friendships. As little girls, we come to recognize the emotions and actions that accompany jealousy, and by the time we're adults, we're so used to sitting with jealousy that we can begin to fail to notice its presence, especially in our own thoughts and actions.

Four of us hit the road and headed south for spring break on our way to visit a fifth friend we'd gone to school with. She was my roommate but had withdrawn after a tough sophomore year of battling depression, weight management, and illness. Since leaving our college, she'd enrolled elsewhere, still pursuing her education degree, had met a guy, and had quickly become engaged. This friend was planning to marry that July, and I was to be a bridesmaid in the wedding.

We arrived at our destination after eight hours on the road and greeted our friend with hugs and squeals.

We descended onto her bedroom and the living room area that was to be our space for the week. It didn't take long before our belongings were everywhere—half-filled suitcases spilling makeup, sundresses and bikinis, fashion magazines, hair dryers and hot rollers; backpacks stuffed with notebooks and textbooks. We slept three to the king-size bed in the bedroom, with two relegated each night to the sleeper sofa in the living room.

Halfway through the week, all was going well. Each morning as soon as we woke up, chaos ensued, as five girls got bikini-ready in one bathroom. We packed lunches and then fought beach traffic for thirty minutes to stake our claim on the white sandy shores. We were determined not to return to school without a tan— evidence of our time at the beach. Evenings we went out to dinner at local chain restaurants, then hung out at the house watching movies, playing Trivial Pursuit, and planning a lingerie shower for our engaged friend the last night we were in town. Invitations had gone out to her local friends several weeks before we got there, and it was looking to be a big party.

One late night, after probably too much revelry, some tension crept in between me and one of the girls. This girl was one of my best friends and the one I'd known the longest. But the next morning she started behaving very differently toward me, even expressing

anger verbally as we all discussed plans for the day. As
the day wore on, the tension became greater. She hardly
spoke to me and began to pal around with the other
girls, attempting to leave me out.

I did indeed feel left out. I immediately knew
something was different, but I was not at all sure where
the chill was coming from or why. I was tortured the
entire day, my feelings hurt. That night I heard my
friend on the phone with her dad saying she was ready
to come home, but I didn't understand what had
soured. We still had half the week to go, and now I
was miserable too, also wanting to go home.

Late that night my friend said something that
pushed me past what I could stand. I can't remember
now what it was, but as everyone fell off to sleep, I
crept out of bed and ended up heaped on the bathroom floor in tears. I stayed there for some time until
there was a soft knock on the door. I opened it to see
her standing there, her face, too, stained with tears.

She came in and sat beside me on the cold tile.
We didn't say anything at first. We both knew there
was something wrong between us.

Finally she broke the silence. "I'm sorry," she
began. "I know I was being weird to you today. I guess
I'm just jealous." I looked at her in surprise, and she
continued. "I am jealous that you're in the wedding

and of the friendship you've maintained over the distance that I haven't."

I was taken aback by her disclosure. I'd never sensed jealousy from her before. To me it seemed baffling; she always seemed so confident, and everyone loved her. We all thought she was beautiful and smart, and we enjoyed her friendship enormously. Everyone wanted to be her friend—everyone always had, in all the years I'd known her. We made up that night, of course, both assuring the other of our friendship. I finally slept, my heart no longer heavy with tension and rejection, and the next morning our friendship resumed its normal rhythm.

Have you been there? Probably. As little girls, we're jealous over attention from a teacher, clothes, friends, and toys. As adolescents, we're jealous over attention from a boy, clothes, friends, and stuff—from iPods, cell phones, and bedroom décor to popularity and freedoms. As women, we're still jealous of attention from someone: a boss, a man, a friend; we're jealous over clothes, bodies, homes, children, income, relationships, and successes.

Rather than getting better with age, jealousy seems only to get worse, and there are simply more things to feel jealous about. I remember as a little girl in the first grade being jealous that my friend Christine had bubblegum that was shaped and colored like a bologna sandwich, complete with bubblegum lettuce, tomato, and the works. Ah, for the simpler times!

The authors of *Midlife Crisis at 30*, Lia Macko and Kerry Rubin, confess in their book the solemn pact they made not to tell any of their friends about their book idea until the ink was dry on the deal. Emerging from a meeting with a publishing executive, they sensed this was going to go places—their ideas had clearly resonated. As they tell it, Lia and Kerry scouted a place where they could quietly clink champagne glasses. But after sharing the news with respective boyfriend and husband, Lia and Kerry realized they could not do the same with friends and colleagues. Their experience had taught them about the damage that can occur to relationships and potential successes when jealousy rears its ugly head. When the deal was signed, the women found their reticence was indeed validated; the reaction from friends was neither delight nor congratulations but instead looked a lot like jealousy over another woman's success.[5]

Jealousy is the stuff of historical stories, movies, and soap operas—from what's gone on between biblical characters like Rachel and Leah to the travails of fairy-tale favorites like Cinderella and Snow White and soap-opera happenings on *General Hospital* and the reality show *The Bachelor*. There's drama between the villains and climax in the relational tension. But most of us don't act out our jealousy by poisoning an apple or making a play for another woman's husband. Instead, our jealousy is far more subtle and secretive.

But is that really progress? How much better is the ugly underbelly of emotion that lives only in the darkness of shadows, lurking and waiting? Jealousy feeds off negative thoughts like pond scum until it festers and grows and, bubbling up from the darkness, spills over us, polluting our thoughts, our motives, even our actions.

The truth is, at some time we all feel jealousy. It's the little wistful pang that happens in your heart when you wish that it, whatever *it* is, was happening to you, that someone's life was yours, or even that you had what they have. The thing about jealousy, though, is that it is so much more than wanting a possession to add to a cache of other items; it goes beyond wanting an experience to tick off the list or bragging rights to something. The painful, even dangerous, thing about jealousy, assuming we are not actually poisoning apples or trying to take someone out with our car, is all the feeling behind it.

Have you ever found it difficult to be happy for a friend because you were jealous? Or been secretly relieved when her budding romance went belly up or she didn't get the promotion she was expecting after all? Are you just a little bit pleased when something finally goes wrong in her seemingly charmed life? Do you feel minutely better when you see the cracks in your friend's perfect marriage?

While paying for my purchases at a clothing boutique, I listened to the conversation between two female sales associates as they folded and bagged my new clothes. "A girl I went to high school with came in here today," one associate said.

"Really?"

"Yeah, she's gained so much weight. She's bigger than me now, and she was really skinny in high school. It made me so happy." She giggled in triumph.

"Why does that make you happy?" the associate countered, to my surprise.

Why does this kind of thing make us happy? I thought as I slid my credit card back into my wallet and walked away with my purchases.

Simply put: we just feel better. Maybe because we cease to feel so defective; we see the too-perfect cut down to size— our size. Or perhaps we want to be seen as the better woman, not merely comparable. We want others to be jealous of *us*.

What is behind these feelings of jealousy? Are we jealous of a happy marriage because we are struggling through our own? Do we feel like we're not good enough, unloved, or a failure at achieving the life we so desperately wanted?

Jealousy survives only on our feelings of inadequacy. Dissatisfaction with the imperfections of our bodies, the things we want in life that seem out of reach, the rewards we think we deserve but aren't getting, and all that we've worked hard to get that yet eludes us—these are the nutrients that give gestation and eventual life to jealousy. We find ourselves thinking and doing things that we regret.

Jealousy is not an emotion that makes us feel good about ourselves either. It's not a socially acceptable emotion. Sure, we all acknowledge that jealousy commonly exists, and most of us would admit being the target of someone else's jealousy. But though we all actually feel jealous at one time or another, few admit to true jealousy, and rare is the case if they do. We joke about jealousy or use it as a compliment. We tell someone that we're so jealous because she's going on vacation or so jealous of her new car. But this use of the word is socially acceptable and no one thinks much of it.

In real jealousy, there is shame. It's an emotion that makes us feel small, petty, and insecure, an emotion that drives people to extreme behaviors. (And who wants to be identified as one of those psycho girls we all love to hate?)

So instead we don't face our shameful feelings; we don't explore actions we can take to move beyond these feelings of jealousy. We let them fester, we act out against our friends, and we feel generally rotten about them and ourselves. These feelings, if ignored, poison our hearts and perhaps, too, our friendships. And as a result, we do painful things like shoving our big foot into a tiny and much-too-tight glass slipper.

THE OLYMPIAN FRIEND

With every conversation, every choice, we grasp for first place; jealousy drives us to do, to strive for, to act out. Competition is what causes eating disorders to spread across college campuses, sells fashion and beauty magazines, and drives us to determine how we look and feel by how others look and feel. Competition is the axis on which our economy and our culture spin. In the end, rather than connectedness, competition creates isolation as secrets are kept and truths are hidden to prevent infiltration.

When female friendships turn competitive, they're no longer places of safe refuge. We become fearful about sharing successes or ideas with friends and fearful about sharing disappointments too. When did we as a gender start to see one another as competition? Is it because we're seeking the approval of men, because we desire beauty or want to have the best? Or is it power we want? Is it because we want power and by being the most of something, or even simply just more than someone else, we can win?

How long we have been competing against each other, I'm not certain, but this I know: the dynamic of woman against woman is nothing new. In her book *At the Root of This Longing,* Carol Lee Flinders traces it back at least three thousand years.

By the second millennium BC, commercial prostitution

in Assyria had taken its place in society and looked to be there to stay. Historians surmise this was really an outcome of slavery as developed through kingdom conquests and also "debt slavery," meaning that those who had gotten themselves in a financial pickle could offer their wives or daughters to pay off their debts.

As prostitution emerged as an industry, the government deemed it necessary to better define the demarcation between the classes. Women became commodities and sex became profitable, and thus the need arose to differentiate the virgins from the prostitutes. In an effort to be clear about which women were sexually available and which were being kept for a rainy day, so to speak, a law (Middle Assyrian Law 40) stated that wives, daughters, and widows of gentlemen must wear veils in public. Prostitutes and female slaves were not required to wear them; in fact, they were forbidden to wear them and would be punished for doing so. By this law a woman no longer had control over her own body; she could not choose to give or withhold it. The law drew a line, separating woman from woman. It divided women and alienated them from one another by provoking competition for who was the most valuable, who could draw the higher price. And so as a woman of class looked into the face of a prostitute, she did so through a veil that clouded her vision and acted as a boundary between her and her sister.

"And how that line has persisted!" says Flinders. "It redraws itself in the life of every girl and woman, starting, for most of us, sometime during junior high school."[6]

Do we, like the Assyrian women, compete with one another about value and our own sense of it? Is our competition much like the economic law of supply and demand? If few women are as desirable as we are, then does our value go up?

But in whose eyes does that value rise? A potential partner's? God's? Other women's?

We can win the best man, the best job, and the best life—the greatest blessings in reward for first place—but in the end we stand in the winner's circle alone, because success won by competition means running solo and having to watch your back. Someone with a quicker stride is always breathing down your neck.

THE MARIE BARONE FRIEND

Marie Barone is, of course, the mother in the sitcom *Everybody Loves Raymond,* the one who undermines her daughter-in-law at every turn, while staunchly claiming only innocent intentions—ah, passive aggression. Jealousy and competition nearly always pass the baton to passive aggression in friendship.

Why passive, though?

I watched my little ten-year-old friend Ashlyn in her karate practice one afternoon. The students were learning to take their partners down to the floor, defeating them by pinning them to the ground, body on top of body. As her instructor barked commands, the kids practiced the technique with their partners. I noted with intrigued amusement that Ashlyn, a very talented and practiced black belt, and her female partner, also a recent black belt, looked unnatural and awkward as they attempted to force the other down to the floor. Meanwhile, the boys in the class were quite comfortable with at least the idea of the technique, if not the finesse.

I concluded that this difference was due to the fact that the boys were actually used to playing that way—aggressive and physical—whereas the girls were not. This is key. It seems that women have no socially approved way to express aggression, so they use manipulative and underhanded tactics. Girls are programmed to keep social harmony, according to Brizendine in *The Female Brain*. To the female brain, keeping the peace is a matter of life and death, and from the earliest days, typical girls live most comfortably in the realm of harmonious interpersonal connections.

"They prefer to avoid conflict because discord puts them at odds with their urge to stay connected, to gain approval and nurture," Brizendine says. "Aggression can push others away, and that would undermine the goal of the female brain."[7] Though both men and women exhibit aggression as a means of survival, it is far more subtle in women.

Carol Gilligan supports this theory in her book *In a Different Voice*: "If aggression is tied, as women perceive, to the fracture of human connection, then the activities of care…are the activities that make the social world safe, by avoiding isolation and preventing aggression rather than by seeking rules to limit its extent."[8]

Still, conflict exists in all of our relationships, but likely out of fear we direct our responses in a passive-aggressive manner. And most likely we've all acted this way and been a receiver of this behavior too. No one can deliver a zinger while suggesting ignorance the way a woman can. A seemingly innocent comment, layered with insult and laced with judgment yet dressed up to look casual, can do the trick nicely if you're looking to put a "friend" in the place you think she belongs.

Those who are especially good at this can deliver a barb so smoothly you're really not sure whether they're passive aggressive or merely unthinking and insensitive. We've all heard a disparaging comment, sarcasm, or disdain from another woman directed toward someone else's life or situation— someone not present, of course, but someone whose situation resembles our own closely enough to leave us wondering about the intent.

If verbal manipulation is not your forte or weapon of choice, there is the silent treatment, rumor spreading, or social jockeying to make sure the person you intend to offend feels pushed to the outside of an inner circle. We invite friends to lunch and don't include one person, or we make public that we were chosen to be privy to a conversation that others weren't part of, or we repeat unkind gossip, as told to us by someone else, to the subject herself. Of course, we're off the hook because we're just reporting what we heard and can feign innocence. We use body language to communicate positions of power, displeasure, or rejection. The way we fold our arms, toss our heads, and make eye contact can communicate what we want to convey.

I remember that when I was a little girl and mad at my younger sister, I would wait until she looked at me and then quickly snap my head to look the other way. I'd repeat this behavior to the poor child multiple times to make sure she got the message that I was mad at her and therefore refusing to look at her. It was juvenile, certainly, and I feel terrible about it now, but I think I've seen the adult equivalent go down many times—when a friend gives someone the text and cell phone silent treatment after a disagreement or purposely mentions in front of someone an after-hours get-together with co-workers to which that person was intentionally not invited.

Does this behavior sound like junior high? You bet. That's where we practiced our skills. But walk the halls of any office and you'll discover it there too. From the school cafeteria to an office conference room, it seems only the geography changes. The behavior stays the same.

A Gallup survey found that 60 percent of eighteen- to twenty-nine-year-olds would rather work for a man than a woman.[9] People probably have this preference because, as another survey reported, woman-to-woman office sabotage has increased by 50 percent during the past ten years.[10]

Donald Sharpstein, a psychologist who conducted an in-depth study of workplace power dynamics, concluded that women are far more likely to use gossip for revenge than men are.[11] I would think this is why most women before arousing conflict with another woman will first connect themselves to a third woman. Again, go back to junior high days. Remember how rarely a girl would launch an attack on another without having her clique behind her? And if the conflict was between two girls in the same clique, you can be sure one was campaigning in the group like an expert politician, using gossip and rumor tactics to ensure support before going on the attack.

The cruelest part about passive aggression is when we act this way toward a friend. You know her, love her, and therefore hold an even greater arsenal of methods with which to draw blood. How can we love a friend so genuinely and yet at the same time sink our lances so deeply into her already wounded areas?

We've all played a starring role, haven't we? Or at the least we've played opposite a real drama queen. Yet I think we would all agree it's time for a curtain call.

THREE

The Lesson of Lucy Van Pelt

The voice bursts through the phone as soon as she picks up the receiver. "Guess what I just heard!"

"Hello?" she says quizzically and laughs.

But the voice on the other end of the line ignores her response and continues. The news is too good. "You're going to die when I tell you. I promised I wouldn't say anything, but I just *have* to tell someone," the caller persists.

Does she hesitate for just a second before asking what the news is? Does she politely find a way to tell her friend to keep her promise and keep her secret or try to steer the speaker toward something else? She does none of those things. Instead, she walks to the sofa, kicks off her heels, tucks her feet underneath her, and gets comfortable. Pulling a cushion under her arm for support, she slightly lowers and deepens her voice in conspiracy and says, "What? Tell me."

This may sound like a familiar conversation. If you think your friends are talking about you, you're most likely right. In an article on MSNBC.com titled "Psst! Gossip May Be Good for You," Linda Carroll, referencing a study published in the *Journal of Applied Social Psychology,* writes, "People generally were willing to share damaging, negative personal information when it involved a same sex rival. And they'd happily pass on good news only if it was about a friend."[1]

Let's face it, we all gossip.

Truman Capote was famous for it, as are Lucy Van Pelt of *Peanuts* fame, Joan Rivers, and Cindy Brady. We do it at dinner parties, Bible studies, family get-togethers, and department meetings. We gossip in restaurants, in the car, on the phone, and via e-mail. Gossip is the entire content of magazines, television shows, and comedic stand-up routines. And as women we've been talking about one another practically since we could speak.

Says the author of *Queen Bees and Wannabes,* Rosalind Wiseman, "Gossip is one of the fundamental weapons that girls use to humiliate each other and reinforce their own social status."[2] You may recall the movie *Mean Girls.* Based on Wiseman's book, the dark comedy exposes a clique of popular girls, the Plastics, and their weapon of choice, which was a self-published book of gossip about their fellow students and teachers.

Given that we've been sharpening our gossiping skills since we were adolescent girls, it's almost impossible to stop, Wiseman says. "While gossip still has the ability to ruin your day, its impact on your adult life is usually superficial and fleeting."[3]

I don't completely agree. Gossip most certainly can have a greater than superficial impact on you as an adult. More than ruin your day, it can ruin your friendships.

Why do we enjoy talking about each other so much? Why does it entertain us so to dish about our friends, acquaintances, people we don't much care for, and, worse, even people we actually care a great deal for? Common sense (and our mothers) tells us that if one friend gossips to us about another, then we can be sure she's talking about us to someone as well. So why do we do it? What are we getting out of breaking confidences, and why are we finding satisfaction in people's disappointments? Is it that we feel better about our own disappointments? Do we think that there's a limited amount of happiness and, if someone else has it, our chances become less? Why is gossip like a car wreck that we just can't stop rubbernecking at? There's something so satisfying about it.

Two friends, heads close together, laughing and sharing confidences—that's just good fun; let's admit it. And many who feel guilty about the overt gossip session find ways to sugarcoat the digs. In the south we even have a phrase to finish off a catty comment or judgmental gossip; just to make it go down easier, we punctuate every statement with "Bless her heart."

If you're not from the south, it goes something like this: "Since Anne Marie put on all that weight, she just looks poured into those pants. Someone needs to tell her those look terrible, bless her heart." Or, "Poor Donna Jo's husband has been cheating on her with his secretary, though I can't say I'm surprised. Men like women who cook for them, and she was always a dreadful cook, bless her heart." Add the word "little" and you can get away with saying even worse. "Shelby's wedding was sweet. Such a shame it will never last, bless her little heart." You get the idea.

Does all this talk of gossip sound like an hour of *General Hospital*? Perhaps, but it could also sound like an hour of women's Bible study, where gossip is often dressed up as prayer requests. One way or the other, most of us find a way to say exactly what we mean. Linda Carroll notes that this comes as no surprise to anthropologist Helen Fisher, a professor at Rutgers University. "It's a leftover from way back when, when humankind still lived on the savannah. Men were out hunting, often alone. Women, on the other hand, needed to raise babies. They needed to build a network. Sharing information about others was a way to start and cement connections."[4]

And certainly that is true. Don't we feel we know Jennifer Aniston better after we read ad nauseam about her breakup with Brad Pitt? And what about Tom and Katie? Connection is forged among the gossipers too. When you get together with friends and everyone talks about someone else, a bonding takes place, especially when you're all in agreement.

Is connection what we're in search of when we talk about the lives of others? Is voyeurism the daughter of loneliness?

Perhaps yes, at times, but I'm not inclined to be so benevolent. I think there's an uglier side to gossip than mere loneliness. Wiseman quotes Jane, an enormously insightful sixteen-year-old, saying, "Gossip is like money. We exchange it, sell it, and lend it out. It's what we have of value."[5] I think she's exactly right, but not only the ability to buy, sell, and exchange—in this current climate, money affords us power as well. From the halls of government and the campaign trail to the slick pages of *Vogue,* corporate boardrooms, PTA meetings, courtrooms, and singles bars—money is power. And so is gossip.

We use gossip to wrangle for position in groups of friends or for leadership at work or on a committee. We use it to gain friends or become the friend favored over the competition. Gossip is a tool we use to win elections and titles. I've used gossip as a conversation starter at a party or when I'm trying to connect with my co-worker who I'm afraid is mad at me and I can't think of how to break the ice. It is a weapon we use to wound someone who has hurt us. And as Christians we use it to gain a moral status over someone else and to make ourselves feel we're looking better than the next person to God or our Sunday-school class. But, questions author Carol Lee Flinders, when it comes to telling tales and drawing lines of distinction to separate women from one another, "If we got the goods on enough of us—on nearly *all* of us—then [isn't] it possible we could just forget the whole line-drawing business and get on with life?"[6]

She was someone I knew only casually. I met her many years ago through mutual friends. She was a teenager then, and really my relationship with her—if you could call it that—was maintained through mutual friends over the years. I'd see her at camp in the summers or at conferences we both attended with our parents. But it was from others that I heard she started dating someone, broke up with her boyfriend, and transferred to another college.

Once, when I was in her city for business, I contacted her, thinking we could meet for dinner or coffee, but that weekend didn't work for her. When she got engaged I was a recipient on a mass e-mail telling friends and family her wonderful news. I hosted a bridal shower for her, and I drove the four hours north-

west of where I lived to attend her wedding. After her
marriage, she moved to the city where I'd grown up
and was now living, and from time to time I'd see her
at parties and events. Whenever I ran into her, she
hugged me tightly—a real hug, not merely a formality
of greeting—and we exchanged surface conversations.

So when my life was crumbling around me, she
was not someone in whom I was confiding. Only those
closest to me were on the need-to-know list. But someone was telling her. An informant who was in the know
was divulging to her the catastrophe that for the time
was my life.

One particular evening she and her husband were
guests at a dinner party. While dining on pork tender-
loin, potatoes au gratin, and asparagus spears, one guest
attempted to contribute to the dinner-table conversation by seasoning it with gossip. In what I'm certain
was mere curiosity rather than malice, he asked another
guest what was happening in my life. Before anyone
could answer the probe, she interjected, with short
sternness that was uncharacteristic for her, "This is not
dinner conversation." She effectively shut down the
topic of conversation before it grew feet and walked.
The evening moved on, and no one broached the subject again.

Naturally, I wasn't there, or the conversation

wouldn't have taken place. But as I'm sure you can guess, someone who attended the dinner party relayed the events to me for the purpose of alerting me to the fact that someone had broken my confidence. I don't know that I can really describe how I felt when I heard the story. Hot embarrassment, suspicion, enormous respect, anger, conviction, and gratefulness surged through me all at once. And above all what I felt was instant connection. I felt a connection to her, instantly closer than I ever had in all the years I'd known her. And at the same time, I felt shame—shame for all the moments when I took someone else's personal pain and made it dinner-table fodder or when I treated callously something that was meaningful and profoundly important to someone else—and deep regret for when I had previously treated heartache as news.

Sure, "everyone will have forgotten it by tomorrow," our mothers told us. True, the humiliation will probably only last until the next victim is hung on the gossip gallows, but the damage to friendship and to character lingers much longer than the latest news flash. And so if connection is what we're after, are we going about it the wrong way?

What if connection becomes greater by keeping secrets and sharing something personal to you rather than sharing what is personal to an absent other? What if power comes from empowering others rather than dominating them? What if friendship is cemented by rescuing a friend's reputation when it may be on the line? What if the glue that holds us together is discretion, not disclosure?

And what if trust is the life that courses through the veins of our relationships?

FOUR

Betrayal by Burger

The goal was not to leave until she agreed to check into a hospital with us—or at least be evaluated. It was my first intervention—and my last to date. To be honest, I didn't want to do it. I was not the confrontational type, but girls who were far more educated about anorexia than I, who knew more of the signs and how to handle it, talked me into it. I cared for her, though, and was certainly concerned about her.

In restaurants she'd order a few vegetable sides and then push the food around on her plate without really taking a bite. She ran religiously. She was always training for a race, the next 5K, and then it was marathons, but she didn't eat more to compensate for the arduous training. And we were essentially standing by and watching her whittle down her once-healthy five-foot-eight frame more and more.

I felt that I wouldn't be a good friend to her if I didn't participate in this group confrontation, though I didn't want to do it. I was afraid I was turning a blind eye to her condition, looking the other way because it was more comfortable for me.

We made plans with her for dinner one weeknight, an ironic mistake we somehow missed in our best intentions. After meeting ahead of time, we showed up at her place as planned. And she was ready to go as promised, but we said we wanted to talk to her instead. And there was an additional member with us, someone older and not usually in our circle of friends, which immediately hinted to her that something was up.

I saw the surprise in her eyes, the uneasiness in her body language, and instantly I felt we were betraying her. We sat on the overstuffed L-shaped sofa and each took a turn, trying gently to tell her our concerns and reading Scripture verses to back up what we were saying. When it was my turn, I told her my concern for her. I tried to dress up my words in terms of fear and worry rather than judgment and accusation. I told her I feared what would happen to her, and I read a verse to support my desire for her life.

She was blindsided, and she must have felt so

alone. In the past year she'd been through the death of her mother, then many months later the breakup of an engagement. She had always struggled with eating disorders and issues of body image and self-esteem. It made sense that an eating disorder would rise like a creature from the deep out of the ocean of grief she'd been treading in for months and months.

Under duress from the four of us, she agreed to go and talk to a counselor at a center that had the option of inpatient care. But she'd have to consent to inpatient care, and I knew there was no way she would. She grabbed her purse and keys and headed for the door but not before throwing over her shoulder a sarcastic remark about thinking she'd be eating dinner that night and now wouldn't because we were making her go to the center. She was right, and sneakily we'd eaten burgers before meeting her. I felt sick about it at the time, the cheese and meat sitting like a rock in the pit of my stomach, a reminder of my betrayal.

We arrived at the center. She signed in, then disappeared into the back with a counselor while the four of us, the supporting friends, waited for hours. And then she emerged triumphant and ever so smug that she passed the intake examination, that she was not anorexic due to a few key items on the checklist that disqualified her. She was practically giddy with self-satisfaction, while we by contrast were discouraged. Not because we wanted her to be unwell, but because now we knew she would not seek help. We felt like failures; we realized that she was well informed and knew what to lie about. We were still worried for her, but there was not much else we could do.

The strange thing is that I felt she took it out on me. My relationship with her was never the same after that. She called me the next day to tell me that she thought my eating habits were the same as hers and, basically, how could I say that about her. It wasn't a heated conversation. I tried to tell her that I only did it out of concern. I don't know if she ever believed me. But there was always an awkwardness between us that was not present with any of the other girls who participated in the intervention. Maybe it was me. Maybe it was my inability to know how to relate after a confrontation such as that one.

We talked from time to time, then less, and finally not at all, though there were multiple reasons for that and we probably both played off the other. I saw her in a shopping mall about a year later, just returned from her honeymoon. She tried to walk right by me until I called her name. She looked back, then stopped, spoke briefly, and told me to call her. I didn't have her number. I never called.

I never talked about the intervention with any of the other girls either. Perhaps there was remorse in all of us, or at least uneasiness as to whether or not we did the right thing. The thing is, I know that every one of us did it for the right reasons. We loved her. We thought we were helping her. I'm still not sure if we did, but I kind of think we didn't.

There are true friends who feel compelled to help when they see a friend in trouble. Their actions require great courage because they may be putting the very friendship on the line to try to save what they believe needs saving. Often, though, the way they go about "helping" makes a painful situation worse or even leaves lasting wounds. Then there are friends who feel it is their calling in life to point out your every flaw, to confront you on anything they see amiss in your life. Seeming to feel their spiritual gift is constructive criticism, they never lack advice on how to be a better girlfriend, wife, employee, mother, or friend. They are always available for an unsolicited pep talk on how to do things better than you're already doing them.

Unintentionally, I overheard a conversation between two people discussing a friend who had left his wife and children for another woman and a new family. She recounted the details of the situation. He listened, asking occasional questions. Both commented on the immorality and selfishness exhibited by the offender, this friend who had left his family. Finally, with all the sordid details uncovered and laid before them, he said to her, "Well, you've told him what you think of what he's doing, right?"

"Oh yes, of course!" came the immediate response.

I stopped listening at that point, but their conversation gave me pause to think. Why do we suppose it's important to voice our opinion about the actions of our friends? Entire books are written and sermons preached about confronting others. Why do we think we should play the role of Holy Spirit, conscience, or conviction? And worse, why are we so quick to enter a verdict and make sure a consequence is levied for the alleged crime someone else might've committed? Why are we concerned that an offender be punished, even when the offense really has nothing to do with us? Are we afraid that silence condones the behavior in question? Do we fear that our friends will think we agree with their choices if we say nothing—that silence will be mistaken for agreement or, worse, encouragement?

Then there are friends of the opposite extreme, who fear confrontation or being the bad guy. They nod or listen, fearing that a backlash would ensue if they were to question or disagree. And there is the friend who, in an effort to be nonjudgmental, suspends opinion, allowing to each her own.

A group of friends were discussing the current well-being

of a mutual friend who was recovering from a severe drug addiction. One in the group noted that he had talked to the absent friend a few days earlier and that the recovering drug addict mentioned that he had been participating in some mild and recreational-only use of a drug that in the past had been his gateway to harder and heavier use of other drugs. In an effort not to pass judgment and, I'm certain, to avoid driving this friend away again, the member of the group apparently said very little in response, though he expressed concern to the group when he recounted the conversation. I was surprised he didn't say more. But since I didn't know the situation intimately, I said nothing.

Are we supposed to confront our friends? If you decide the answer is yes, then how do you do that? How do you speak uninvited and yet candidly without ruining the friendship? When does it cross the line into just being judgmental?

This is a touchy issue among friends. Dietrich Bonhoeffer said, "The truth will make us free, but that truth is always untimely.… We all live in constant, insurmountable fear of the truth, even if we don't know it."[1] It's hard enough to look at ourselves honestly, but when someone else chooses to step in and hold the mirror up to our faces, most often the defenses go up and the arms go out in an effort to push the friend away.

Why do we feel the need to confront people? It's true that we all have blind spots that are visible only to others. If we can see them, then by their nature they are no longer blind spots. Therefore don't we need each other to mirror what we can't see ourselves? But then again, just because we can say something, does that mean we should? A confrontation, even initiated with the best of intentions, can turn quickly, planting seeds that can eventually bring a friendship to rot and ruin, possibly with permanence. Is it our responsibility to confront anyway? And when should we do it? If you don't like your friend's fiancé, is it your responsibility to say so? If your friend complains to you about her husband, what should you say? From admitting that an outfit doesn't look good on her to speaking candidly about destructive behavior, what is our responsibility and obligation as a friend? And what may be situational and open to interpretation?

I was listening to the radio on my commute home from work. Impatiently punching buttons, I looked for something to hold my attention while at a standstill on the overcrowded highway. I ceased surfing when I found a segment called the *Cindy and Ray Show*. As part of the show, people write to Cindy to ask advice, then Cindy reads the scenario over the air and gives her opinion. Afterward people call in and give their opinion about what Cindy said or the problem at hand.

The question I heard raised was, "Should you tell a friend that her boyfriend is cheating on her?" After explaining her justification, Cindy eventually said no, you should not. Her answer surprised me. I would certainly want to know if my boyfriend was cheating on me. But the reason Cindy gave for her answer was that she had told a friend in the past and the friend did not believe her. Seemed like a good enough reason…

Then I started thinking about the scenario. Are we actually responsible for what our friend does with what we say when we confront her? Or are we only responsible for what we say and how we say it? And is it really livable to try to separate the two from each other? If we are considering confronting a friend because we believe by doing so we are genuinely caring for her, should her potential response determine our action? Perhaps that is the distinction between trying to be a conscience and trying to be a friend. Maybe sometimes we confuse the two.

Confrontation and conviction are not the same, nor are we responsible for both. Difficult as it may be to watch someone we love make destructive decisions, we are not responsible for how that person responds to gentle chiding, confrontation, or even the cold, hard facts.

We walked together every evening. It was our way to decompress from our day; we'd get a little exercise and some quality friendship time too. As soon as I got off work, I'd shed my conservative suit and sling-back heels for shorts and running shoes. We'd meet at the nearby high-school track after cross-country and track practices were over. After stretching, lunges, and calf raises, we'd take off on a brisk walk. Our many failed attempts to keep count of how many times we rounded the track resulted from our commitment to talking transparently with each other.

On one of these walks, she told me she had started dating someone. Each subsequent day we talked about her new relationship, and I started to see some patterns in the things she was sharing with me. Red flags went up, and I began to worry. She was making choices in the relationship that were harmful to her and to the man she was dating as well. I wasn't sure what to do.

At first I only listened, unsure what to say, but making sure I didn't verbalize encouragement for what she was doing either. I'd go home after our walks troubled by the conversation and not sure of my role as her friend. What do friends do when they see their friends being self-destructive? Should I tell her what I thought—what I feared? But what if she didn't want to be my friend anymore? I wrestled with the choices, and I prayed about what I should do. Then I remembered that when Jesus encountered individuals who were being judged by much of the community, he only asked questions. Jesus chose this approach rather than shoveling on another heap of conviction.

Unfortunately, rather than suspending judgment,

we often just ask a friend if she wants an order of fries with her condemnation platter. I decided not to say anything, and I determined instead that my approach, too, would be to ask questions. (And no, not the questions my mother asks when she wants me to do something or doesn't want me to do something—not questions like, "When is your next haircut?" or, "Are you going to wear that?") Instead I tried to ask questions that would remind my friend of what she already knew—to bring to the forefront truths already buried deep within her heart.

For weeks we walked, she talked, and I gently queried. In the end she began to see her actions for what they were and recognized the need for change. And I wholeheartedly supported her in those efforts.

Looking back, I feel I made the right choice in my course of action, for her and for our friendship too. We still walk together every day. The track is our steady circle in all the ups and downs life takes us on. But we still lose track of our laps. Too busy talking, I suppose.

FIVE

For Love of Friendship

Upon leaving dinner, he walks with his remaining friends to
the place called Gethsemane. There he spends the evening
racked with anguish over what lies before him. He makes one
last request of his friends, asking simply that they stay awake
and pray with him. Then he beseeches God, pleading that
what lies ahead of him be removed. He knows full well the
power of the Father; he knows God could choose another
way. He could after all intervene, saving the very life of his
Son and removing the choice he now has to make. Jesus's
emotional distress in this is palpable, even physically evident
in the drops of sweat and blood that bubble up on the surface
of his skin.

Consider what it's like to face a situation that requires an
impossible decision. You are trapped between impossible choice
one and impossible choice two. There is no good option; each

decision is partnered with undesirable consequences. Yet we know that God in his infinite power could reconstellate things. God could take that cup, that decision, from you so that the choice would not be yours to make—nor yours to be responsible for. But as a wise voice in my life has said to me many times, "God is a very adult God." And God requires us to be very adult too.

Here God requires the unthinkable of Jesus, and one last time he begs for another way out. Who of us wouldn't? But the answer is not relief, only silence.

Jesus returns to his friends, and there they lie, asleep and unaware of his torment. He wakes them and again pleads with them to stay awake and pray. Once more they fall asleep. His time in the garden that night is finished only when his friend Judas betrays him to the Pharisees, even daring to signal the betrayal with an audacious kiss. And the thing about Judas was that he didn't think he was doing the right thing in betraying Jesus. Judas was not a whistle-blower; he was not standing on his principles or making a difficult decision based on misguided convictions. No, he was simply a sellout—and a greedy one.

Hours later in custody of the religious leaders, Jesus is turned over to the Roman soldiers. He will spend the early morning hours being interrogated, beaten, abused, then finally abandoned and killed later that day. But all of that yet lies ahead.

Nearby his friend Peter warms himself by the fire. Peter is frightened, to be sure. He was by the side of Jesus at his arrest. He saw the betrayal of Judas, witnessed the kiss, and when they tried to take Jesus, Peter alone fought in defense of his friend, lashing out and cutting off the ear of a servant of the high priest. But now he fears for the life of his friend and for his own life, too, because of his association.

Perhaps driven by the instinct of survival, he does the only thing he thinks he can—or maybe he doesn't even think. He disassociates himself and denies, not only once but three times, that he even knows Jesus, let alone is his friend. And as soon as he does it, Peter catches sight of Jesus and realizes his friend knows of the betrayal.

Imagine the look on the face of Jesus when he locked eyes with Peter. His dark and soulful eyes were most likely filled with crushing hurt. Here, no one could help him but God—and God would not. Jesus was completely alone. I wonder, did he feel like everything he had given to Peter was all for nothing? Did their days together, the laughter, the exchange of ideas, the travel, the miracles, Jesus healing the man lowered through the roof, Peter walking on water toward Jesus—did all those life-altering moments mean anything? Were they wasted, unappreciated, or forgotten, reduced to nothing in a moment of betrayal?

All these thoughts could have flooded the mind of Jesus in less than a second when he met the eyes of his guilty friend, having just heard Peter deny even knowing him. And Peter! Imagine the guilt that flooded through him. We are told that he went outside and wept bitterly. I am sure he was racked with sobs until there was nothing more to cry, and he probably doubted he could ever ask for forgiveness or make it right. He would remain haunted by those dark, sad eyes that witnessed his betrayal, and he could never attempt to explain or justify his fear, his unthinking, his denial.

Inasmuch as the sharing of souls and lives is the fabric of friendship, another thread too must be woven throughout the pattern of our relationships. For the life force of friendship is twofold: it is love, and it is also forgiveness, unconditional and infinite.

Mere days after the crucifixion of Jesus, all was once again right in Peter's world. Jesus was back with the disciples again. Once more they talked together. And once again together on the shores of Galilee, Jesus asked Peter if he loved him. Did Peter shift uncomfortably? Did his mind dart back to the night of the betrayal and wonder if Jesus was thinking of that too? How many times, I wonder, had Peter revisited that night in his mind?

Jesus, undeterred, asked three times if Peter loved him. The first two times he used the word *agape,* which means "universal love," a love that lacks favorites. But the third and final time, he asked the fisherman something different. When Jesus asked Peter if he loved him, Jesus used the word *philia,* the word for friendship love. This love is far more intimate than agape. Friendship love speaks of knowledge of the object of our love. It speaks of community, partnership, commitment, service, trust. Friendship love speaks of listening, honesty, forgiveness, giving the benefit of the doubt, and sacrifice. It is standing and declaring publicly, "This is my friend."

When Jesus acted on philia love, he laid down his life for his friends. "Greater love has no one than this, that he lay down his life for his friends."[1]

Why did Jesus ask Peter if he loved him? Was Jesus looking for reassurance or wanting to make sure Peter felt sufficiently guilty? Or did he want to convey that he still wanted Peter's friendship? Perhaps one of those motives was behind the question, but what is also clear is that he had forgiven Peter for his betrayal. We know this because Jesus taught Peter about forgiveness too, when the disciple asked how many times someone should forgive.

Does every great friendship experience betrayal? Should we all expect to be betrayed by our friends at some point?

The Women, a 2008 movie remade from the original 1939 version, brings life to the friendship of four women in midlife. Two of the women—one a magazine editor, the other the wife of a notable and highly successful businessman—date their friendship back to early college days. When the other two joined to create a foursome is not clear. The narrative really begins when three of the friends discover that the successful businessman is cheating on his wife, their beloved friend.

As viewers, we follow the wife's story closely as, within the protective circle of her friendships, she attempts to respond to and recover from the reality of betrayal within her marriage. The story takes a dramatic turn, though, when, in a desperate effort to salvage her faltering magazine career, one friend leaks the intimate details of the marital betrayal to a local gossip magazine, thus committing an unforgivable betrayal of her own. The friends part ways for a time, and if not for the suspicion that this movie will end as many do—happily ever after—we wonder if their friendship can be restored. And of course it is, but only after the two college friends share an impassioned conversation, part confession and part accusation, in which the betrayer contends to her wounded friend that all relationships will know a betrayal.

The reality is sobering for both the characters and the viewer. But if it's true that all relationships will know a betrayal, what does this truth require of us? I suppose it asks that we grow up, that we cast aside a naiveté that told us we could love unscathed, and that we forgive.

I still have much to learn about forgiveness. To be honest, forgiveness can be a struggle for me. Shamefully, I can tell you that I have held grudges for wrongs. I have let friendships dwindle away over being hurt, betrayed, or simply disappointed. And perhaps I was right to step back some from those friendships. But were there those I left behind simply because I did not want to forgive or did not know how? Forgiveness is something we learn by doing, and perhaps it often eludes understanding until we are called undeniably to act upon it.

In 1994 nearly one million Tutsi lives were brutally ended in merely one hundred days. In a devastating act of genocide, Hutu extremists systematically and brutally massacred Tutsis (as well as many Hutus). The Hutu militia destroyed men, women, and children; students died in their classrooms; entire families were snuffed out. Rwanda's rolling green hills were bathed in blood. Photographer Annie Leibovitz captured chilling images of an empty classroom splattered in blood, red handprints and footprints still identifiable. Much has been written and discussed about the Rwandan government's involvement or lack thereof. Those in positions of power in our country and the world over ignored warnings of the impending genocide. Many reasons probably could be given for the lack of involvement, for doing nothing while an entire segment of humanity was targeted. I have not personally spoken to anyone who had foreknowledge or was in a position to do something, so I don't know the truth. I only have my own idea of the truth, which is that world leaders probably saw Rwanda as insignificant in the global and political landscape. The faceless people probably made it easier for those in positions of power to ignore the information and intelligence that came across their highly lacquered mahogany desks.

And yet the Rwandans who survived have an inexplicable mercy and grace that we could learn the world over. If we were to learn forgiveness from the Tutsis, the impact would be unimaginable.

After her 2007 visit to Rwanda, my sister relayed to me the story of a documentary, *Rwanda Rising,* about the aftermath of the genocide. The film tells how the surviving families of the victims were assigned the task of trying Hutu individuals in the courts of their own villages. The magnitude of the atrocity and the number of those who had to stand trial for their alleged roles in it were too great for any one court, so it was determined that each alleged murderer would stand trial in the village of those killed at the murderer's hands, standing face to face with the victims' remaining family members or community. One would expect conviction after conviction from such biased juries. The documentary reports that instead, in a show of mercy most assuredly incomprehensible, the villages are choosing in many cases to forgive rather than kill again. Instead of capital punishment for their atrocities, these offenders have received grace and forgiveness from the families and friends of those they so brutally destroyed.

I don't really know all that much about that kind of forgiveness. I have withheld forgiveness for wrongs of infinitely less enormity. Forgiveness of the magnitude shown by the Rwandans is far beyond many of our understandings. To be honest, the forgiveness Jesus showed to Peter is beyond comprehension as well.

What makes forgiveness difficult? I suppose the memory of the wrong lingers, and so does the hurt. Perhaps we are fearful that the wrong will go unpunished and that the one who hurt us won't realize the depth of our hurt. Maybe if she is forgiven, she won't regret what she did as long as we believe she should. By the act of forgiveness, are we giving up a grudge that is our right to bear? And perhaps we are afraid of being hurt again.

But ensuring punishment isn't our responsibility. Jesus didn't work that shift and doesn't require us to do so either. And we will be hurt again. There is nothing safe about relationships, and there is nothing safe about forgiveness either. Jesus himself went to a cross in the name of forgiveness. Forgiveness requires much from us, we know that. And so does love. If we are to love as Jesus loved, it is in spite of fear and with all that love demands.

In his essay "The Joy of Two," Christopher Bamford says of the interaction between Jesus and Peter, "More than letting go of offences, forgiveness achieves consubstantiality. To forgive is to humble oneself before the other, to serve the other, to place the other before oneself. It is to overcome all that comes between oneself and the other—all the ego's defense strategies, all contra-dictions, contra-thoughts, contra-feelings.... Only then," he continues, "can one co-speak with one voice."[2]

We forgive because, yes, we know we are asked to do so. But we forgive because we desire restoration and, ultimately, because we are in need of salvation. We forgive because, if all relationships bear a betrayal of some kind, then eventually we, too, will be in need of forgiveness. We forgive because we have already been forgiven.

SIX

The Age of Friendship

I liked her right away, but I never dreamed we'd become friends. A year later, though, she showed up for her freshman year of college at the school where I was already a sophomore. Eventually we became friends, then roommates. We talked about boys, love, feminism, our bodies, our dreams, our fears. We shared clothes, earrings, and nail polish. She talked more than I did, opened up more than I did, though I wasn't aware of it then.

In college she was evolving. She was trying desperately, though with some uncertainty, to shed her innocence, her preppiness, the vanilla image of a girl raised in a conservative, Christian, and southern home. She simply wanted to make her own way in the world, stake her own claim, and she was figuring out exactly what that claim would be. She had difficulty hiding her evolution. The messiness of the process—her uncertainty, her adventure, her attempts and failures—was there for everyone to see. I'm not sure she minded everyone knowing, though. In contrast, I seemed more sure of who I was and where I was going. To her, and to me too, I guess, I seemed more stable. But it turned out that I was a late bloomer and she was my teacher.

She wanted to be the edgy and mysterious intellectual who drank espresso straight up without twisting her face at the bitterness. She was majoring in history and had a crush on her brooding and single professor. She learned how to make cappuccino without needing a thermometer to test the temperature of the steamed milk. It was another trait of an intellectual—the ability to make exceptionally good coffee. She cut her hair; she changed her wardrobe; she went to Europe.

When she came back, she was different, distant for the first time. I think she thought I wouldn't understand her experiences there. Or maybe wouldn't approve. But I think she was more what she wanted to be after Europe. She was no longer naive and inexperienced. I could tell by her walk, her mannerisms, that she felt more worldly. She wanted to paint, write, and philosophize in indie coffee shops or vegan cafés she hunted down and took me to. She drove an old convertible Volkswagen Rabbit. She'd put the top down, shove a Beatles tape into the deck, and we'd drive around singing, "Beep-beep, beep-beep…yeah."

I thought we were friends, best friends. I thought I shared everything with her. She fought for our friendship; I see that now. She would offer advice easily, voice her opinion without fear, but she supported me in my choices, even when many others didn't. Still, she thought our friendship could be so much more than it was. She thought I was stoic and staid. She wanted to know what was behind it all. I insisted there wasn't anything more. But she knew better, and every so often she'd push me for more, finally backing down in discouragement and frustration when she didn't get anywhere with me.

Years later I remembered her insistence that there was an untapped depth to my soul, and I decided to go there and see if she was onto something. And she was.

We're still friends, though distantly. I graduated from college and moved away. She graduated a year later. We got busy with boyfriends, then marriages, juggling careers and children. Now we e-mail from time to time, but we're separated by distance, life experience, and busyness. So I suppose she would say we're casual friends.

She thinks she loves me more than I love her, but I

feel the opposite is true. And sometimes I think that she would be proud of the person I've become. Not because I've accomplished anything great, but because I have gone to another depth within myself and in many of my relationships. It's where she always wanted me to be. Somehow I never understood what she meant until it was too late to be the way we once were in our age of friendship.

Is there an age of friendship? Is there a time when our friendships are richer, deeper, even more in number? As you look back over your years, how have your friendships changed? Was there a time your world revolved around friendships, but now that stage has passed? Do you give the same priority to friendships as you did in earlier years?

There is a time when friendships seem easier, simpler, I suppose, like most of life. We experience a stage when friendships are the center of our world. We eventually trade that world for careers, travel, boyfriends who become husbands, children, and even solitude. As we grow older we become more comfortable with ourselves and we are at ease being alone. And if we aren't content being alone, we transfer our needs to other relationships in our lives.

C. S. Lewis suggests that perhaps we count friendship as the least important love because it is the relationship we freely enter into, then freely maintain. As a society, he says, we place importance on a spouse and family, easily marginalizing the significance of friendship.[1]

We don't need our friends in the way we once did. At least we think we don't. We still do need our friends, of course, but the pursuits of life often get in the way, and the friendship priority tumbles further down the line behind landing the promotion, home-cooked meals, company dinners, soccer practice, swimming lessons, yard work, and laundry.

Are we encouraged to abandon our friendships after we've married? Do we expect to trade friendships for husbands? Certainly, a marriage commitment becomes a high priority, but does entering that commitment mean forsaking all others, even our girlfriends?

In a *Wall Street Journal* article about factors contributing to marital infidelity, Naomi Schaefer Riley writes, "Friendships with members of the same sex generally used to fall by the wayside when people got married or, again, change in scale or importance." Riley quotes Diane Sollee, a former marriage counselor who's now in her sixties, saying about her own generation, "The idea that these friendships would take any priority over your husband was unheard of." But in describing the cultural shift in which married women now give significantly more weight to friendships, Sollee goes on to note that girls' night out and girls-only vacations have become much more common.[2]

Do we feel pressure or obligation to reduce the commitment to our friendships when we find a husband? Perhaps so, though we feel somewhere deep inside that we have made a sacrifice to do so and therefore expect him to do the same. In fact, Lewis says he blames the demise of male friendships on women—or at least on "silly" women.[3] This is the woman who keeps her husband from his friends unless she, too, is there. She resents his time with the guys.

Do we feel insecure or resentful of his guys' night and expect that as we abandon any and all devotion to a relationship outside of marriage, so should he? Contrarily, do we attempt to please the so-called demands of marriage by trying to have our cake and eat it too? Wanting to maintain our friendships, we try to open the circle and implore the men to join.

I think of events as simple as wedding showers or baby showers and how we have tried to change them. Wedding showers used to be for women only and were characterized by conversations, laughter, silly games that were stereotypically female, and delicate sandwiches or petits fours. Then we decided that men, too, needed to experience the fun of showers. But anytime I have been to a couples shower, the men looked so uncomfortable, almost like deer in the headlights. Do they really even want to be there? And what was wrong with showers for women only? Is it perhaps that when we have settled down with family and home, we feel guilty about the friendships we keep?

The ancient traditions of China acknowledged there was indeed an age of friendship. Women were linked to one another as "sworn sisters." These were deep and abiding friendships that always had the expectation of an expiration date. A sworn sisterhood involved membership in a group made up of several girls. The group dissolved at the time of marriage. Sworn sisters would go through foot binding together, learn the trade of womanhood together. Most meetings of sworn sisters took place in the women's upstairs chambers where the women would gather to sew, to write, and to spend time with other women. A man would never venture there. The inside chamber was for women alone to work and to share thoughts with one another. It was understood in Confucian culture that the inner circle of the home was for women alone, as the outer realm was for men. Women did not cross into the outer realm in either thought or deed, so the inner realm was a very important place to express their thoughts, ideas, fears, and even humor. Therefore even one thousand years ago, women's sworn-sister friendships were designed to nurture and bolster them in the demands and expectations the culture placed on them.

From time to time I look back over pieces from my previous friendships: birthday cards, letters, and poems, and photographs of Christmas gift exchanges, homecomings, graduations, and late nights of sleep-deprived hilarity. I look back over those memories with nostalgia. I see myself in those pictures and think how young I was then. Not so much young in years, though I was that, too, but young in life experience and wisdom.

Sometimes I think it's sad that later we get so caught up in the business of living life that we often don't really live life. We spend our time *doing* so that we can eventually start living. But it's not only mere busyness, of course; adult life makes legitimate demands of us. The truth of the matter is that priorities often change; they need to change for the sake of the relationships and responsibilities we have chosen for ourselves. We make new friends at our places of work or our children's school, or with the wives of our husband's friends, and that is certainly not a bad thing.

But we hold the age of friendship with sacredness, if we ever stop to think of it, in part because, though those friendships were the center of our world, we didn't really appreciate them until the age had passed. Even when we are consumed with demands that take priority over friendships, we hold a greater appreciation for those relationships, both past and current. Those friends knew so much more of our lives because we spent so much time together. They saw far more of our ups and downs, our messiness. Often those friends knew us before we learned to conceal our messiness so well. That was when we dreamed about the life we would have, before we actually thought we had it or realized we weren't going to. That was when we thought we could do anything, be anything, accomplish anything, and have everything.

Our friends sat with us when we divulged the exhaustive details of the first date with the man who was later to be our husband, when we realized we hated the major we were two years into, and when we broke off our first serious relationship. They were with us when we had impossibly unreal expectations for our bodies, figured out what we were going to be when we grew up, got our first "real job," bought clothes that weren't on sale, and stepped over the threshold from coed to woman.

But I'm starting to think the age of friendship comes back around. "Every real Friendship is a sort of secession, even a rebellion,"[4] says C. S. Lewis. Perhaps later in life we have the courage again to stage that rebellion. We seem to have a renewed appreciation for the age of friendship when it returns the way fashion trends from decades ago do—like capri pants, skinny jeans, and miniskirts. Our friends no longer define us as they once did, but we now choose friends for how we are drawn to them, and they are very much a part of us.

And while the rule of fashion is that one should not attempt to wear a trend when it makes its return the second, or perhaps third, time around, we are never too old for friendships. In the second age of friendship, our friends sit beside us as we struggle to keep a marriage fresh and alive and champion us when we finally get the promotion to senior management or purchase the home we'll probably live in for the next few decades of our lives. They engage with us as we rethink so much of what we thought was true about life when we were younger. And later they come alongside us as we care for aging parents, as our children leave us, when we learn we have breast cancer, and as we maneuver grandparenting and adjust to being around young children again. These are the friends we live life alongside with a sense of humor, having finally learned that we just can't take ourselves too seriously anymore, the way we once did.

In the tender first age of friendships, those girls were our lives, but in the second age, they are women who help us navigate what has actually become our lives.

SEVEN

Soul Friend

I was thirteen that summer, and so was she. We would become best friends. My parents had started going to a new church not long before, and that meant forced youth group attendance for me. Joining a youth group and trying to break into the cliques as the new kid was torture as far as I was concerned, but I wasn't really given the option of not going.

I had been attending the youth group for a few weeks and still felt awkward and unsure of myself. It was Sunday night, and I was leaving church with my parents. She was standing by the door, coordinating rides for other teenagers who were still too young to drive.

"We're going to Whitney's to watch a movie and eat pizza. Do you want to come?" she asked me sweetly.

I couldn't believe she was talking to me. She was beautiful and cool, and I felt awkward and dorky.

I somehow communicated that yes, I wanted to go. "Good," she said. And then she added, "If you want, you can just spend the night at my house and then your parents don't have to worry about picking you up tonight." After my parents granted permission, I readily agreed to the plan. I went to Whitney's, just as we agreed.

After the movie we went back to her house. We talked most of the night and listened quietly to Z93 on her clock radio—a music station neither of us was allowed to listen to—until we fell asleep. I slept on a trundle bed that pulled out from underneath her twin bed. She told me her parents were strict and that she was going to redecorate her room and paint it black and white. I felt honored she confided this to me. I couldn't believe she wanted to be my friend.

Chocolate, beaches, and Mexican food—these are a few of my favorite things. My sister and I were musing together the other day about favorites. More specifically we were talking about being the favorite, being someone's favorite person. Our conversation was about being the best, the one and only person to hold that place of honor in someone's life—anyone's life.

"Do you think that's something we should ever want?" she asked me. "Or is it something we're never meant to have?"

"I don't know," I answered her thoughtfully. And then I confided something I'd never told anyone, perhaps because of the obvious narcissism it revealed. I told her that when I was a little girl, it always bothered me that I could never be God's favorite. No matter how good I was, how well I obeyed my parents, how much I shared with my sister and brother, how regularly I prayed, or how many verses I memorized for Sunday school, God would never love me, nor even just like me, better than anyone else he created. I would never get to heaven, look into the face of God, and hear God whisper in my ear, "You were always the most special to me of everyone."

Together my sister and I laughed at my childish angst. She found my disenchantment humorous, but she was hardly surprised; she vividly remembered the pensive child I was. While most little girls drifted off to sleep hugging a Cabbage Patch Kid or Care Bear, I lay in bed at night in my Strawberry Shortcake pajamas, bothered that God didn't and wouldn't favor me, no matter what I did. And even as I recount this story again for the purpose of this chapter, I am fully aware of the audacity to even want such a thing! I could dismiss it, I suppose, and wave away the unattractive image by reminding myself (and you) that I was eight years old.

But my desire to be the favorite didn't end with God. I desperately wanted to be the teachers' favorite too. I remember being in kindergarten and wanting to invite my teacher to my house for dinner. Years later I was thrilled when called upon by a teacher to run an errand for her during our fifth-grade science fair. My teacher did not typically call on me to run errands, and as she told me what she wanted me to do, I was only too eager to help, hoping this was a sign of a new beginning. As I trekked to another classroom to deliver her message to another teacher, I envisioned being the go-to girl going forward. I was sure she'd see how well I accomplished her task and I would be the favorite errand runner.

Truth be told, I still would like to be the favorite. If we're honest, don't we all? Don't we want to be someone's best girl?

Whether or not we're *supposed* to want to be someone's favorite, I don't know, but it is something we *do* want, often very much. Every little girl—and perhaps even not-so-little girls—seeks one coveted place of honor. It is the honor of best friend. From elementary school BFFs (best friends forever), to teacher's pets, fiancés, and maids of honor, we want to be at the top of the heap in someone's world. We want to know that, above all the other girls in the class or in the clique, we are the favored, the best girl in someone's eyes.

Even the twelve disciples of Jesus clamored to be his favorite when they asked who would sit at his right hand. And yet Jesus is antifavorite. Because, I learned as a child, if you're looking to be someone's favorite, you won't find what you're looking for from God. You may recall John 3:16, the well-

known verse we find splashed everywhere from baseball sta-
diums to graffiti-embellished highway overpasses: "For God
so loved the world." Yes, *the world.*

Sure, God loves you, wholly and truly, but God loves the
sinner right beside you just as much. God loves the man who
cut you off in traffic, the kid who screamed the duration of
your flight, the woman in front of you in Starbucks this
morning who took the last pumpkin scone, and even the co-
worker who ratted you out to your boss last week for your
perpetual lateness.

No matter what you do, God will not love you more than
anyone else, and you cannot be his favorite, no matter how
hard you seek that position or how perfect you are. Now I
realize this is actually good news, but what do we do with this
longing to be the favorite?

I so wanted to be a favorite. And then I was. I had a best
friend, and I was someone's best friend as well. Jennifer was
my best friend. Our houses stood side by side, making it convenient to play together nearly every single day. She was
already home from Montessori school when the bus dropped
me off on the corner just across the street from my house. I'd
run home, change out of my gray and black plaid uniform,
kneesocks, and loafers. After quickly stepping into corduroys
or jeans and a T-shirt, I'd bound across my yard to hers or
watch her run to mine.

I bossed her around all the time, but she didn't seem to

mind. We had a best-friends necklace. It was a gold chain with a pendant of half a heart. My half was engraved,

be

frie

for

Her necklace was exactly the same, except she had the other half of the heart that read,

st

nds

ever

We shared a tree house that her grandfather built for us right along our property line, and we both had a younger sister and a baby brother. We watched *Annie* a thousand times, I think. We had sleepovers on Friday nights, and I played with Barbie dolls at her house, which I wasn't allowed to do at mine. Jennifer had the dream house and the convertible. After her mother took us to see *Cats,* she liked to belt out a nasal version of "Memory" at her parents' dinner parties or school talent shows.

She was my partner in crime, though the crimes were usually some brilliant plan I thought up that went awry. We got yelled at once by a very cross elderly lady for cutting down all the morning glories at the nursing home Jennifer's parents owned—my idea again. I thought they were beautiful and wanted to bring them inside. Her mom just laughed when she found out. All of this made us best friends, I suppose. But then my parents moved away when I was ten. I saw her once after we moved, when her family came to the city we were living in, but never again. I had other best friends later; I even had other necklaces. I'm quite sure she probably did too.

Being a best friend was a very important role as a little girl. It was one we all took seriously. "The best-friend relationships girls have in early adolescence can be the most intense relationships girls will ever have," writes Rosalind Wiseman in *Queen Bees and Wannabes*. She describes the relationship as two girls who are truly inseparable. Their worlds revolve around one another. They share their own languages and codes, clothes, and toys. Often they will even have a crush on the same boy.[1]

In elementary school and middle school, you just had to have a best friend, if only for tactical reasons. And it was sufficiently devastating if you got un-best-friended, perhaps for the new girl in your class or someone with a cooler Trapper Keeper. As important as the title was, we used it to manipulate and punish as much as to reward, didn't we? Does something like, "If you go to her party, then you're not my best friend!" sound vaguely familiar? Back then best friends were often as easily cast aside as scratchy wool turtlenecks in May when someone cooler or more convenient came along.

It was the first week of school. Caleb sat quietly and subdued in the backseat of his mother's SUV, looking out the window. He had enjoyed nursery school and was excited about joining his friends in kindergarten this year, so his behavior seemed odd. His mother glanced back at him through the rearview mirror and caught sight of his pensive expression.

"Caleb," she called to the back of the Yukon without taking her eyes off the road, "how was school?"

"Alex says he doesn't want to be my best friend anymore." The confession out there, he sat back against the seat, sighed, and looked out the window again.

She wanted to ring Alex's little neck! Every cell in her body felt for her little son in his loss and rejection. And instinctively I put my hand to my heart, wincing in pain at Caleb's rejection, when she told the story to me.

We remember how it felt all too well. As children and even as adults, we know the sting of the loss of friendship. We still yearn for friendships and mourn their loss. And even as adults, though we may not wear the divided-heart necklace to prove it, we still have best friends.

I don't remember actually learning what a best friend was. I just remember we talked about best friends and invited someone to be our best friend. I don't remember ever needing an explanation about what that meant. As we grow older we no longer formally extend the invitation; it becomes one of those things you just know.

If best friendships back then were about playmates, secrets, and asserting yourself as the center of someone's world through bossiness and social positions, what characterizes our best friendships now? What drives us to both bestow and seek such an honor? Perhaps the position goes to the childhood friend or the friend we've been through the most with, the one we feel safest with. She is the friend who knows all about us and loves us anyway. The friendship is characterized by trust and forgiveness. Either time or experience, or both, has proven her friendship.

Even if we grow out of bestowing the actual title of best friend on those who are deserving, there is still a best friend who sits on the throne in our hearts. And if the throne should become vacant, we move through life fully aware of that empty space within us.

The idea of best friends is an ancient concept. Friendship was a vital part of the tradition of the early Celtic Christians, its critical importance having originated with the Desert Christians, monastic ministers in the barren desert lands of Egypt, Syria, and Palestine during the third through fifth centuries. The Desert Christians ultimately inspired the Celtic Christians in their practice of soul friendship or *anamchara*.

The ministry of soul friendships was a very important aspect of Celtic spirituality. Their spiritual teachings placed great significance on opening one's heart to another, on confessing sin to another, and on mentoring another. The model of friendship and its importance greatly affected the modern world and how we view soul friendship today.

Writes Edward C. Sellner in his book *The Celtic Soul Friend*, "Soul friendship also affected the entire history of Christian spirituality, affirming as it did the conviction that a person's relationship with God can take the form of effective dialogue, and that whenever sins or faults, grief or human vulnerability are openly and honestly acknowledged, healing begins and God's presence is experienced, sometimes unforgettably."[2] The effect was so great that the idea of Celtic soul friendship made its way into the seven sacraments of the Roman Catholic Church, those of spiritual healing, as well as into part of the practice of the twelve-step program used by Alcoholics Anonymous. According to Sellner, the modern psychological and therapeutic counseling professions today find their roots in the ministry of Celtic soul friendship.

Much is written about this early Celtic tradition and the importance the Celts placed on friendship. They laughed and lived together, sharing humor, work, and spiritual thoughts and expressions, baring their hearts and souls to each other in sacred friendship. The Desert Christians taught that all people must open their hearts and that self-disclosure was good for the soul. With vulnerability and transparency they shared their doubts, fears, sins, and spiritual journeys with each other. Practicing a nomadic lifestyle in the desert, these early Christians had very little in possessions and wealth. Living in shared space, often with a "room" mate, their lives were devoted entirely to survival, spiritual awakening and growth, and relationships. This practice birthed the soul friendship that was so vital to the early Celtic church.

Sellner notes with significance that they anchored the importance of friendship in the person of Jesus. Their commitment to friendships and the sacredness they attributed to the soul friendship were rooted in the memory of Jesus, as evidenced in the poignant call of an early Celtic father, Abba Theodore: "Let us each give his heart to the other, carrying the Cross of Christ."[3]

The Celtic Christians give us an exquisitely beautiful picture of friendship that resonates deep within our souls today. It is friendship with others and also with God. In the expression of soul friendship they articulated for us, we recognize the deep longing to share what is on our hearts with other human hearts. And this is why we long for a best friend.

We long for a best friend as we long for home, for comfort, for love, and for acceptance. What makes this woman our best friend is the trust we place in her when we share our heart's deepest hurts and disappointments, our questions or success, our dreams, and our laughter. It is our best friend who will scour the depths of our hurt and disappointment with us. It is our best friend who celebrates our joys, who gives answers to our questions. Sometimes, even more important, it is our best friend—our anamchara—who sits in the unknowing and the fog with us, not pretending to know.

Spiritual writer Henri Nouwen said, "When we honestly

ask ourselves which persons in our lives mean the most to us, we often find that it is those who, instead of giving much advice, solutions, or cures, have chosen rather to share our pain and touch our wounds with a gentle and tender hand. The friend who can be silent with us in a moment of despair or confusion, who can stay with us in an hour of grief and bereavement, who can tolerate not-knowing, not-curing, not-healing and face with us the reality of our powerlessness, that is the friend who cares."[4]

And so perhaps the concept of best friend is not so much about favorites. It is not simply a position, an award, or a status. Perhaps it is really about belonging.

I was sitting in a nail salon, drying my freshly manicured hands and admiring the Hey Vito, Is My Car Red-y? paint on my fingernails. I glanced around the room, people watching and passing the time inside my head while sitting under the nail dryer. A woman hobbled over with wet toenails and fingernails and settled herself, with the assistance of a nail technician, at the nail dryer across from me. As she set her purse beside her and perched her keys next to the dryer, I absent-mindedly took in her blue jeans, her tunic-style cotton top, and the black wedged flip-flops she would slide her feet into after her toenails were dry, and I began wondering what her life was like. I caught sight of an engagement ring and wedding band adorning her left hand, and I felt an instant pang of jealousy pierce my heart.

My thoughts immediately leaped from her life to my own, and I explored that trail of jealousy in my five remaining minutes under the dryer. I was in love, perfectly contented in my romantic relationship, even a little wary of the perils of marriage. So where on earth did that jealousy emerge from?

It was belonging, I realized. It seemed as though her ring said to me, *I belong to someone. When I leave here, I go to a house and a home where I belong to another.* Her ring was proof of this. Bear in mind that by *belonging* I do not mean ownership. Belonging to another does not mean the other person possesses you. Rather it is about a connection, a partnership, a grounding. To be anchored to another keeps you on the course of your journey, connecting you to your own sense of value and meaning.

And as with the wedding ring, we look for symbols and proof, tangible expressions of our belonging. A passport says, "I belong to this country." Membership or baptism in a church says, "I am part of this institution, this community of believers." A Girl Scout's uniform says she is part of the Girl Scouts of the USA and has access to Thin Mints, and a closer look at the uniform reveals she belongs to a specific troop too. A gym membership says, "I belong here and have access to its privileges." Even my American Express card has the inaugural date of my membership stamped on it. We label our belongings by name. Last names identify us as distinct from someone else who shares the same first name. They give us a place in our family history, and, most important, they connect us with others in belonging, in family.

After my divorce I chose not to return to my maiden name. I had several reasons for making this decision, mostly practical. But after it was final, I had some shadowy moments of doubt over my decision as I struggled with belonging. My name gave me no sense of belonging to anyone. I no longer carried the name of my family of origin, but I also had no connection to my married family anymore, though I still carried the name.

Seeing the woman in the nail salon made me realize that, for all its perplexities and risks, I wanted marriage because it meant belonging. And I don't think I'm alone in that desire. Regardless of how it sometimes may appear, marriage is more than sexual permission, doubled bank accounts, and acquiescence to a social institution. People get married because they are looking to belong. We seek out relationships with others for the same reason.

Our hearts find a home in our best friend because we are only looking to belong, to anchor. Even as children, when we seek out a best friend, we hunt until we find the one person we want to make a pact of friendship with, and then we belong. In the end it seems it is not about being the favorite as much as knowing you can count on this person, that she is there for you, and that your souls are connected. In the adolescent terrain of social expectations, in-crowds and out-crowds, party invitations, and the lunchroom cafeteria walk of shame, we are saved by that best friend, the familiar face and place, and we belong with someone.

When we grow older, only the stakes change, and perhaps the labels too, but our longing is much the same. Our need to tether our hearts to a soul friend only grows deeper as we grow older. Years of experience only bring a deeper awareness to our longing to belong.

In truth she was my favorite from the day she was born. I anticipated her arrival without really knowing what I was waiting for. And then she was here, a tiny bundle of blankets with a shock of dark hair peeking out.

From the beginning she was loving, affectionate, happy, and adventurous—a real ham. She made me laugh until my stomach hurt, even when she wasn't trying. I bossed her around like I did all my other friends, I tattled on her, and I always made her share her carefully rationed leftover Halloween candy in January when mine was long gone and Easter still far off.

Back then I took our friendship for granted. It was easy and convenient. I had a built-in friend for family vacations; a willing playmate for playing house, dentist, and hairdresser; and a costar for the Christmas Nativity play I took it upon myself to direct.

But somewhere between adolescence, then college days and long distance, boyfriends, other friends, careers, and even husbands, it became a soul friendship—it still is. It is full disclosure, confession, sharing deep wounds and slow healing. It is the exchange of ideas, sharing doubts, learning, teaching, laughing until literally crying—a laughter that ripples through your entire body until, when it has finally subsided, it leaves you feeling cleansed, lighter on your feet. It is an understanding that runs so deep it has even surprised us. It is a secret language, a sentence completed by the other, a look that says a million things when words can't be used. It is the occasional fight, bouts of competitiveness, jealousy, and disappointments, followed by unofficial cooling periods, unspoken forgiveness, and then things returning to normal easiness. It's a phone call for fashion advice, romantic wisdom, shopaholic confessions that you couldn't tell anyone else, or needing to borrow confidence, faith, or a sweater. It's being quiet or never running out of words on a twelve-hour road trip.

Sure, she's my sister, but that's not what made us soul friends. Not all sisters are best friends. It's all the expressions and experiences that define our best friendships, and then we wake up one day realizing we belong to a soul friend. It's being a favorite, having a favorite, and having a friend who knows you like no other.

EIGHT

Light and Mirrors

She arrived looking coolly casual in black shorts and
a royal blue sleeveless blouse that set off her hair color,
just the way I remembered her—chic, but seemingly
effortlessly so. Slender, tall, and with olive skin tanned
in late summer, she moved with grace and elegance.
I wished I looked like her, moved like her.

Lunch was nice, if a bit awkward because we didn't
know each other that well. But the friendship had potential; I could see that. I was trying to play the part
of knowledgeable host, introducing her to my haunts
and places I frequented. Afterward I went shopping, in
search of outfits that would mimic her relaxed style.

We started to spend more and more time together,
the two of us and with our significant others as well.
I introduced her to my other friends and felt a pang of

jealousy when they seemed to hit it off extremely well. Our friendship seemed good, and we were becoming closer, but I always felt a certain presence. It was the presence of competition. She seemed to compete with me in passive ways. When I became engaged before she did, she dropped a few indirect comments about her having dated her boyfriend longer and therefore should be engaged first. As I planned my wedding, she seemed threatened. When I mentioned restaurants I wanted to try, she made reservations and ate there first. Rather than a desire to share our experiences, there was a sense of one-upmanship.

We continued to spend time together, but when I shared my successes with her—a promotion at work or an opportunity for travel—I felt her lack of genuine enthusiasm. Worse, when I shared disappointments she seemed to receive the news with a degree of smugness. She eventually became engaged too and began to incorporate details and venues into her wedding celebration that I was not able to use in mine, though I had wanted to. It was at this time I started to distance myself from her, beginning to doubt her friendship. I felt she had a love-hate relationship with me, and that made me feel unsafe.

To me a friend who was envious, who was celebrating my disappointments and regretting my successes rather than the reverse, was not a trustworthy friend. I began to develop a strong aversion to jealousy and competition, climbing onto my soapbox with increased frequency to deliver speeches about how friends who are jealous are not real friends.

And then a wise voice cautioned me to give awareness to my strong aversions. "Perhaps," she murmured, "you are seeing the ugliness of your own jealousy and competitive nature mirrored in your friend." Stung by her suggestion, I met her words with silence. But inwardly I erected a wall around the idea and refused to enter the brier patch her words suggested. I argued and maintained within myself that my own jealousy and competitive nature were created by the presence of hers, as could happen to anyone in my situation. It was a long time before I agreed to look into the mirror at my own image, though its presence nagged me.

I allowed the friendship to drift away. Today, though we live in the same city, I am not part of her life, nor is she a presence in mine. I am certain my observations about her were accurate, but I am equally certain that the observations of my wise friend were correct as well. And heeding the wisdom she spoke to me, I eventually looked, really looked, into the mirror.

When I was ten years old, I had the chickenpox. Being a little past the typical age for this affliction, I had a pretty severe case. I was a week into my illness, running a high fever and miserable with the constant itching. Having finished my daily oatmeal soak to relieve some of the discomfort, I decided to look in the mirror, something I had not done since I discovered my first pock. After stepping out of the tub, I shuffled gingerly over to the sink to stand before the mirror. I was utterly horrified at what I saw. Every part of my face was covered with sores that looked like little blisters. I looked so completely diseased I wanted to recoil, and yet at the same time, I couldn't stop looking at the image in the mirror until I burst into tears over my ugliness.

We see our reflection in mirrors all around us, in nature, our very bodies, music, and art. "Art wants to create individuals," writes John O'Donohue.[1] When music—whether lyrics, notes, moods, or rhythms—resonates within us, we glimpse ourselves, our souls. Says O'Donohue of classical music, "The friendship with this music is slow at the beginning. Like any great friendship, the more you let yourself into it, the deeper you belong. It calms the soul, awakens the heart.... You begin to sense your own eternity in the echoes of your soul."[2]

For centuries stories, too, have been used as mirrors to teach us about ourselves, to show us the world, to show us God, and to reveal to us our own humanity. Jesus taught by using parables that have become familiar to us, even culturally iconic. As a child, I learned that chalky antibiotics in pill form went down much more easily mixed with a spoonful of peanut butter. Similarly, children are actually able to grasp complex ideas well above their development level if the concepts are concealed in a story. And as children we learned from fables and fairy tales about honesty, loyalty, self-control, and patience. Through these stories we were meant to see into our hearts with greater depth and clarity and take both note and action. The purpose of teaching through parables is that the listener will find resonance, then go and be or do likewise.

The prophet Nathan used a powerful parable to reflect King David's action back to him. After David, in his desire for Bathsheba, successfully arranged to have her husband killed on the front line of battle, Nathan went before the king. He told a story of a rich man who had a large number of sheep and cattle and a poor man who had only one lamb. Rather than kill the lamb, he had raised it as a pet with his children. Much like the little toy dogs that are all the rage today, the lamb drank from his cup and even slept in the man's arms. One evening a guest arrived at the home of the rich man. For whatever reason the rich man was loath to take from his own abundant herds of sheep and cattle to feed his guest. Instead he demanded the little lamb from the poor man. When Nathan finished his story, King David was livid over the actions of the rich man—only to look in the mirror held for him by Nathan and see the truth about himself.[3]

When our bodies mirror our souls, we can become physically ill with anxiety, and we can grow thinner with sadness or depression or fatter when we're happy. When we are afraid, our heart pounds; when we're in love, our stomach seems to thrill with us in flips and turns. When we feel nervous, our body temperature rises. And the faces of mothers and lovers seem to truly glow from the warmth within.

The cycle of death and life in nature mirrors the miracle of resurrection in us. So as we leave this world in death and are to be resurrected to new life, we see the cycle of death and life all around us. It is autumn as I write this, the week of Thanksgiving. The trees still burst with color, but with each blustery day, more leaves fall from spindly branches to the ground and crunch under our feet as we walk over them. When the leaves have fallen, the trees will be naked and exposed, and throughout winter they remain barren and lifeless for seemingly endless months. Only to be resurrected to life again in early spring as tiny green buds appear along the branches. Soon this new life will bloom, and the trees will be green and full once more.

But what about another kind of mirroring? What happens when you see your own reflection in the face of another? There is an actual process of the brain called mirroring. It is the ability to read facial expressions, nuances, body language, and tone of voice and actually mirror what the other person is thinking or feeling. If you're reading insincerity, passive aggression, jealousy, or competition, you may very well be correct, and you've understood the emotion or motivation through the process of mirroring.

We can all read another's feelings by mirroring them, but scientists speculate that female brains may hold more mirror neurons than male brains.[4] Essentially, the mirroring is what we call women's intuition, and it enables us to read another's unspoken communication. You may be able to tell when someone is lying or embarrassed and when someone feels threatened, angry, or offended, even if the person believes he or she is not communicating the feelings. We know that a mirror reflects what is looking into its surface, but in this type of mirroring, you are the mirror. You are reflecting someone else.

Rumi, the thirteenth-century Persian poet and theologian, wrote extensively on love and friendship. His most notable work, *The Masnavi,* is a six-volume poem within which he writes of a reunion between Joseph and a childhood friend. Through the story the poem speaks of the important function of mirroring and friendship. At the friend's prompting, Joseph talks of much that happened to him, from his brothers' jealousy to his eventual imprisonment. Finally, tired, I suppose, of reliving the memories of those dark days, Joseph changes the subject and teasingly asks his visitor what gifts he has brought. The guest responds by telling Joseph how he searched far and wide in search of a gift for his friend, the man who now had everything. Just imagine having to bring a host gift for Joseph.

"You don't take gold down into a goldmine, or a drop of
water to the Sea of Oman!" says the friend as he regales Joseph
with the tale of his search, building the drama of suspense as
to what gift he has brought the friend of his youth.

"You have all seeds in your barn. You even have my love
and my soul, so I can't even bring those.

"I've brought you a mirror. Look at yourself,
and remember me."

He took the mirror out from his robe
where he was hiding it.

What is the mirror of being?
Non-being. Always bring a mirror of non-existence
as a gift. Any other present is foolish.

Let the poor man look deep into generosity.
Let bread see a hungry man.
Let kindling behold a spark from the flint.

An empty mirror and your worst destructive habits,
when they are held up to each other,
that's when real making begins.
That's what art and crafting are.

A tailor needs a torn garment to practice his expertise.
The trunks of trees must be cut and cut again
so they can be used for fine carpentry.

Your doctor must have a broken leg to doctor.
Your defects are the ways that glory gets manifested.
Whoever sees clearly what is diseased in himself
begins to gallop on the way.

There is nothing worse
than thinking you are well enough.
More than anything, self-complacency
blocks the workmanship.[5]

But is it possible that in the mirror held before you, through the image of another person, you will glimpse a part of yourself previously unseen? Perhaps of all the mirrors we peer into, a relationship is the most powerful. It is, after all, "the nature of humans to be present in a way that impinges on and engages others."[6] Can the story of another life, a friend, reveal ourselves to us?

In any relationship someone can cause us to suddenly see something of ourselves, whether the relationship is with a co-worker or business associate, a family member, or even a near stranger. But the closer the relationship and the more time you spend with someone, the greater the likelihood this person may become a mirror for you, reflecting the good, the bad, and the ugly. And so friendships especially experience this type of mirroring and offer the gift of seeing a clearer vision of who you are, warts and beauty spots alike.

Assuredly, this mirroring can at times be a gift as desirable as an x-ray showing a broken leg. The news is not good. It is not a pretty picture. Especially when we see our own image by becoming aware of the judgments we administer to others. The sharpness of this clarity can cut like a shard of glass.

Are you vehemently put off by someone you think is a gossip or self-righteous? Do you find a strong reaction within yourself to a friend who is overly critical, selfish, or hypocritical? Of course these traits are not ones that any of us enjoy or try to emulate. So I don't believe that every objection to something unkind or undesirable necessarily mirrors the same in us. Rather, in my own experiences, the degree of my reaction can offer insight into what may be at its source.

After spending much time with a friend who I believed frequently behaved in a self-righteous and judgmental manner to others, I began to dislike spending time with her. I became hypersensitive to her seemingly constant judgment of others and, at the same time, her smugness regarding her own spirituality and life choices. It began to bother me so intensely that I thought about it all the time, even when I wasn't with her. It was so under my skin that I couldn't forget about her attitude even when I was no longer witnessing it or listening to it. And it disturbed me greatly that she couldn't see it, that she was so oblivious to her treatment of others.

That is when I realized the need to take a deeper look into the reflection. Was there something that needed my attention and thought? Was I, too, parading my own spirituality and righteousness around while judging others? Did I need to get the log out of my own eye so that I could see my reflection for what it was?

Truthfully, this is neither an easy nor a pleasant thing to do. Back-to-back morning visits to the gynecologist and the dentist is perhaps an experience that could be likened to sitting with yourself in the reality of your own muck and mire. And most likely that is why we are hesitant to do so. We are masters of denial with ourselves, aren't we?

I have marveled at my own ability to justify my actions or feelings. And I only recognized that tendency by looking in another mirror—that of David, as he bares his soul in his psalms. Throughout his psalms he waffles between confessing his sin, declaring his wretchedness, and acknowledging himself as undeserving of God's grace, and, at the other extreme, declaring his righteousness and ticking off his good deeds, which, he thinks, make him deserving of grace. As I read the verses of David, something rang true and familiar to me. I saw this same expression in myself, in my ability to justify my worthiness of God's blessings to me and his answering my prayers as I declared my own righteousness.

But thankfully, not all mirroring has to be so painful, though even when it's not, it can be equally life changing. I was enjoying lunch with new friends, having made their acquaintance only days earlier. As one in the group spoke of his adventures, there was something affecting in his stories. I wasn't quite sure yet what it was. But something wouldn't let go of me. The more I spent time with my new friend, the more it all felt familiar. He treated me differently than most of my friends did. He wasn't affected by the trappings of my life—my connections and my experiences—as so many were. Something told me that when he looked at me, he saw only me, and I dared to look then too, into the looking glass that he provided.

I saw myself there, but it was an image I'd never seen. In all the conversations, the stories, even the silences I shared with him, I recognized a passion to his life that was mirrored in my own, only I had buried it deep within. He lived with a passion and a grace that I did not. It was there inside me and so it seemed familiar, but I was not living it. Eventually life got busier and we saw less of each other, but our friendship remained and I could not shake the image I'd seen of myself.

I was changed by the memory of it and could not erase its image, this brief glimpse of the self with whom I was not yet familiar, from my mind. I sat with it; I slept with it; I even cried with it. And then I tried to make it real. I suppose it was courage that I mustered to live it, not only see it. It was an unexpected gift from my new friend, only I'm pretty sure he never even realized what he had done.

And this mirroring is one of the many aspects of friendship that is often so serendipitously startling and yet so beautiful. The unfolding of how we were created to need one another, to need our relationships with one another, in order to live fully into the people we were intended and created to be is magnificently masterful. And even when mirroring forces me to peer into some ugliness, I am amazed at the beauty of how this opportunity for growth is revealed to me as I engage in friendships with others.

What becomes so clear is how much we need one another, not in a codependent way but rather to bring to light what we cannot see or perhaps do not want to see. And when we finally recognize our own reflection, we are greater for having done so.

NINE

Surprised by Friendship

A recluse, she lived deep in the woods, a mile from the road and down a dirt path. I was introduced to her because she could no longer manage the onerous effort of caring for the grounds her house sat upon. She hired me, a woman, because she distrusted men and permitted only women to perform any task for her, no matter how strenuous. I found out later she'd never married but had been frequently preyed upon by men who wanted to take from her what they could. Her disdain and distrust of the gender as a whole meant that she was pleased when I agreed to take on the work.

She was reclusive by choice, venturing from her home just once each week to buy groceries, and I was instantly intrigued by her, confident the story of her past would prove remarkable. But there was virtually no opportunity to know her. She met me at her front door when I finished mowing her lawn, opening the door barely enough to push an envelope containing money through the space. Then she would simply murmur, "Thank you. I'll see you again next week."

After weeks of the same routine, she opened the door a little farther one day, and when she handed me the envelope, she asked if I could help her with a bit of housecleaning. I agreed, assuming it would be only the single time. On the contrary, she wanted regular help, and it became a three-days-a-week job.

She was a difficult master to serve. Very particular, a perfectionist, she would check my completed work and make it clear when I did not meet her expectations. I silently quit every day, telling myself I would not be back, only to return as she expected. She was hardened, cold even, but she seemed to like my being there. Little by little she spoke of her past, and I began to learn the fascinating story of this remarkable woman.

Born to a highly affluent Jewish family in Prague, she grew up on a palatial estate assisted by a governess and nannies, a chauffeur, a butler, a butcher, and an entire kitchen staff. Her summer home was in the country, situated on ninety acres of pristine property a little over an hour outside of Prague. She attended an exclusive girls school in the city and spent many evenings at classical music concerts with her mother and father, brother, and grandparents.

Well educated as she was, she was fluent in five languages. Her native language was Czech, of course, but her nannies spoke to her in German, her governess spoke to her in French, and she learned to speak English in school, picking up Spanish later, "just for fun," she told me with a pleased expression.

She was eighteen years old when political unrest crept into Europe. It was 1939; Hitler's rantings were growing increasingly mad, and then it came. The Holocaust happened. Lives were irrevocably changed, hers among them. The Nazis seized her beautiful home and used its exquisite rooms as a headquarters for the German army. Many of her family members were taken, tortured, and killed. Leaving behind her charming city, her friends, her school, the much-loved country home, her beloved culture, and her entire life as she'd known it, she escaped with her parents and brother, bound for America. Surviving for weeks in the cargo hull of a carrier ship, she braved enemy waters, with very little to eat, and arrived finally in the United States, where she would stay for the remainder of her life. She never returned to her beloved Prague. She attended the Boston Conservatory, continuing her education and completing a degree in music education. Later she taught music, French, and English at a school in New Jersey.

When I came to know her, she had ceased a social life of any kind. She attended no more concerts; the only music in her life came from a small record player. She loved animals, though. She loved them more than people. Too many people had wounded her, I suppose. I imagine it's nearly impossible to still believe there is good in people after what she lived through. Her exterior was icy and hard, but inside I was sure there was a vulnerability in her spirit. I believed her heart was still full of desires, and I hoped I could become her friend.

What is it that draws us to unexpected friendships? Though they often surprise us in the way they unfold, there is something unspoken, a feeling or an essence, that draws us to these people, no matter how unlikely. Perhaps we are simply intrigued by their differences; perhaps they become convenient in time and place. Is it that we are desperate for a friendship, or does a soul connection reveal itself in spite of disparate exteriors?

This particular unlikely friendship became a story of unexpected twists.

Two years had passed since I had met her, and I was still
visiting her home to clean or mow the lawn every other
day. Then she learned she had breast cancer. I hoped
the news would allow her heart to thaw, but she only
became harder, angrier. I tried to tell her about my
faith, hoping it would bring comfort to her, but she
would dismiss my words as nonsense. She knew the
Old Testament well; if I ever misquoted anything,
she'd immediately correct me. She had studied many
religions but had no regard for any of them. And as her
cancer advanced, she began to consider euthanasia as an
option. She requested information from the office of
Dr. Jack Kevorkian. The literature arrived at her home,
and she pored meticulously through all of it. I feared
I would arrive at her home one day and find her gone.
I was sure she would take her own life to end her suffering. She didn't, though I never knew what changed her
mind.

As her health deteriorated she could no longer
make her weekly trip to buy groceries, so she asked me
to take her. One day, for no particular reason, we drove
my van rather than her car. I helped her up into the
van, then went around to the other side to slide into
the driver's seat. When I turned the ignition, the radio
instantly screamed from the front speakers, startling us

both. Sure she'd be angry, I reached quickly to snap it off.

She stopped me. "Who is that speaking?" It was a woman's voice, and she spoke with a European accent. Perhaps the accent took her momentarily back to her country she'd left so many years before. In any event, she was intrigued. She asked how often the speaker came on the air and then abruptly changed the subject when I answered. A short time later she asked me to take her to buy a radio.

As time passed cancer ravaged its way through her body. She became bedridden and I, her sole caregiver.

One chilly fall evening, the sky already inky with night, I reached from my chair by her bedside and switched on the radio. There was another voice, another accent. His voice had a note of elegance, and she was mesmerized. As he spoke, she listened intently. And suddenly, with a rage from deep within, from a heart that had witnessed enormous loss and suffering, she screamed at the voice on the radio to prove there was a God and that she was one of his chosen.

As her health deteriorated rapidly, I attempted to ask her about eternity, about God's love for her. But she would only change the subject, as if I had not spoken. She continued to listen to the radio, though. She suffered great pain, and hospice people came to tend to her. All the while the radio station played on, the voices she had grown to love speaking to her from the small box beside her bed. Finally she was unable to speak. Even the ability to shake or nod her head was gone.

One afternoon I sat beside her and spoke softly to my friend. Taking her small, graceful hand in mine, I told her many things. I thanked her for what she had given to me. I thanked her for opening her life to me, for allowing me to trespass even in her distant yet painful and private memories. And then I spoke to her about God. I asked her if in her heart she considered him. I felt her squeeze my hand once. That was our code for yes. I asked if I could pray with her. Again I felt the gentle pressure of her delicate fingers enclosed in mine. And as I prayed, tears trickled slowly from the outside corners of her closed eyes, tracing the outline of her ears before settling into the pillow that cradled her head. Twenty minutes later she lost consciousness and never regained it. The next day her soul drifted away, finally at peace, finally well. Finally home.

Unexpected friendships, unanticipated joy. Even for the cynical soul, life still offers surprises. Some relationships slowly tiptoe into our lives, into our experiences, and into our memories forever, and yet they knock us from our feet with the force of their friendship.

I called the lady who told me this story to request her permission to retell it. Incredibly, the day I made my phone call was the ten-year anniversary of her friend and employer's passing. As we talked, I heard tears in her voice as she recalled the memory of her friend. Truly this unlikely friendship had forever changed both women.

Whether Thelma and Louise, Charlotte and Wilbur, Dorothy and the Scarecrow, or an opinionated English teacher and a spoiled king—we love to be surprised by unexpected pairings. We cheer them on despite the seemingly insurmountable odds stacked against them, delighted by the way they defy the cultural expectations around them and how they stick with each other to the end, even the bitter end for some.

What is it about those friendships we love? Perhaps it's the rebel in all of us, who gets such enormous satisfaction out of bucking the system, if only vicariously, or the competitor, who loves the challenge. Could it be the adventurer in us, who thrills to step just outside our immediate world? Or maybe it's the child in all of us, who delights in the surprise of it, or the artist, who finds meaning in beauty discovered in unexpected places. And we envy the intensity of these friendships, perhaps because the pair is unlikely in interests, the places and experiences each one holds in life, or a difference of age. The contrasts weave an exquisite pattern with two entirely different threads, even different materials altogether. Brought together by neither convenience nor expectation, these friendships are formed rather by a deeper connection, the kindred spirit Anne Shirley spoke of.

The friendship of Ruth and Naomi was an unexpected surprise. The story is not long; only three chapters in the Bible tell the powerful friendship of these two women. There was a great famine, and a man and his wife, Naomi, along with their two sons, migrated to another area, Moab, where they could find food. After they had settled in Moab, Naomi's husband died. Here she was in a new land with only her two sons, who I'm certain cared for their widowed mother. Naomi and her sons stayed in Moab, and the two sons eventually took wives.

Then the sons, too, passed away, leaving the women alone. Here were three women in culturally precarious situations, widows connected only by men who were no more. Naomi probably still felt her own loss, living as she did in a foreign land without the support of friends and family.

But then Naomi received word that her homeland once more had food provisions, so she naturally wanted to return to her roots, to all that was familiar, and, I'm sure, to the place that held many memories of better times. The two younger women were to return with her, but as they were leaving,

Naomi abruptly released them, sending them instead back to the home of their mothers. This was not customary. She kissed them both, the three women wept, and Naomi, their matriarch, sent them away with a blessing. Her daughters-in-law offered to stay alongside her, to return with her to her home. Naomi, considering their futures and her hopes for them, insisted they stay. More tears followed as the women grieved at their loss and their parting. Finally one kissed her mother-in-law and bade her good-bye. But Ruth, the other daughter-in-law, held tight to Naomi. She refused to leave, saying, "Don't urge me to leave you or to turn back from you. Where you go I will go, and where you stay I will stay. Your people will be my people and your God my God. Where you die I will die, and there I will be buried." And then as if to seal her pact with Naomi, she said, "May the LORD deal with me, be it ever so severely, if anything but death separates you and me."

For all intents and purposes, she sealed her friendship with Naomi in blood. Theirs was the friendship of laotong and of anamchara, a lifetime commitment of friendship, of wandering, grieving, and giving thanks, only to be buried with one another in the end. Ruth's words sealed a pact of true friendship with the widowed mother of her deceased husband.

The friendship of Ruth and Naomi became a great catalyst in history, both their own personal histories and ours collectively. Out of her commitment to Naomi, Ruth met

Boaz—for were it not for her travels with Naomi, she would never have worked in Boaz's fields. There in the wheat fields, she was treated favorably by him, they married, and together they had a son, thereby sealing part of the lineage of Jesus.[1]

The depth of Ruth and Naomi's friendship was profound—till death. Why do some friendships seem to run a little deeper? Certainly theirs was a relationship characterized by pain and loss, but it must have involved more than that loss, or it would not have sustained itself once their wounds began to heal.

It seems the differences of two unlikely friends create a unique texture in the friendship. And as each speaks into the life of the other, their differences hold the power to bring novelty, innovation, and adventure to their interactions.

We are changed by relationships, and the pairing of two diverse individuals in an unlikely friendship has the power to bring momentous change in both parties. A friend with disparity brings new thoughts and new views of the world and of ourselves. Such a connection deepens our capacity to understand, to relate, and to empathize. We may see what we never thought possible, even taste of what is new. We are not only simply changed, but we are possibly changed for the better.

Do we then go searching to find unexpected friendships, or do they find us? They are divine appointments, I think. I believe in divine appointments because I believe I've experienced them. I've received gifts of friendship that surprised me by how certain people have woven their lives with mine. What extraordinary friendships have textured your own life?

She was there, thirty-one years my senior, breathing in every detail and allowing it to become forever part of her, just in case she was never there again.

It was India. My senses were awakened, I think, for the first time. In a foreign country, I was overwhelmed by the energy, the sounds, and the smells that hung suspended in air thick with moisture. At times it seemed too much to take in, and other times my hungry soul inhaled it ravenously. We shared conversations, and I sensed a familiar spirit that resonated with mine. It was the beginning of many changes that were to come in my life, and it was the beginning of a friendship that would remain constant through all those changes.

It seemed that almost immediately we shared thoughts, ideas, travel experiences, interests, and details that made us who we believed ourselves to be. Later we would share hurts, disappointments, and fears.

Together we are an inexplicable contradiction of great differences and yet uncanny sameness. She speaks wisdom into my life yet makes me feel as though I, too, have wisdom to share. She champions traits, talents, and gifts that are mine but that I never noticed before.

Her childlike fascination with treasures that many hardly even notice—a tiny bird, the pattern in a single leaf, a wild mushroom that avoided the blade of a lawn mower in her backyard—is wildly contagious.

Once after I arrived at her home and rang the doorbell, she quickly ushered me inside her front door, stuck a cold drink in my hand, and hastened me right back outside through her back door to drink in the colors of the sinking sun. We sat on her back porch in rocking chairs, only chirping birds and the distant hum of a lawn mower piercing the summer's silence, and we took it all in. We spoke only when we could no longer see the sun, not daring to interrupt its grand departure.

When I see her delight in the creation around her, I think how it must thrill the heart of God to see one of his creations take such pleasure in another of his making. A surprising friendship indeed, one that has touched my life forever, of this I am certain.

TEN

A Community
of Friendship

A COMMUNITY OF SERVICE

As a little girl and a student in Catholic grade school, I recall being endlessly intrigued by the nuns. Their convent stood adjacent to the school property, and I was insatiably curious about the life these women shared together. I wondered about these women who pledged their lives to God, forsaking the hope of marriage; even in the second grade, I hoped to be married one day, so this was intriguing enough.

But living together, dressing the same—this was equally mysterious. Did they have their own rooms? Did they ever wear anything besides the attire I saw them in every day at school? One day I got my wish and my teacher, Sister Marie Helena, took us on a tour of her convent. It looked, of course, disappointingly normal. We saw the living room, the kitchen, the posted delegation of chores, and the large community table they dined around together.

After my tour I was less intrigued, the mystery removed. I don't remember thinking about convent living much after that. But it has a long and dramatic history, characterized by rebellion, scandal, and negotiation of authority, as well as commitment to God, poverty, and friendship in community.

A notable order of nuns was led by Saint Clare of Assisi. As a girl she met Saint Francis of Assisi and was inspired. Eventually the two became friends, and Clare confided in him her desire to serve God completely and sacrificially. At the age of eighteen, she left her parents' household against their will, shaving her head, and then, in a dramatic turn, Clare staked her claim to her calling as she clung in resistance to an altar while her forbidding family attempted to drag their daughter home. Instead, she declared her commitment, her life in service to God.

The year was 1212, and at the time there were few organized communities of women. After living in several orders, Clare was moved to a home where she could live in silence and prayer. Surprisingly, her sister, Agnes, joined her, then even her mother, and soon several others. They adopted Clare's way of life, uniting themselves in their calling and in friendship. This was the beginning of the order that would be called the Poor Clares, which still exists today.

Through medieval times, daughters, widows, even wives left their families to commit their lives to community living within convents. There were different rules for different orders, and the society of medieval monasticism became fraught with controversy that reflected the greater culture of that time over such issues as social class within convents, authority, and rules. The nuns of one order were forbidden to gossip outside the convent or to tell stories of another nun to any outsider. Another order mandated that no nun should have her own cell or room.

But ultimately the women who entered these communities formed a society of their own making. And it was a society of friendship characterized by service—to God, to the community, and to each other. Clare worked tirelessly in service to her sisters, serving at the table and caring for them when they became ill. The sisters, having renounced all material possessions, went barefoot, and Clare washed their feet when they returned to the convent after serving those outside or begging to finance their few physical needs. She was even known to slip from her bed at night to cover the sisters who had unknowingly kicked off their blankets during sleep.[1]

I'm sure that convent life was filled with much of what plagues any community of women. No doubt there was jealousy, competitiveness, even gossip. Even Clare herself began her seclusion in another convent, a community of the Benedictine order, and did not find it to be right for her. Only when she was given a new start and was joined by other women desiring the same commitments was she able to flourish in her calling. But these communities offered women a haven from perhaps being married off to men they had no regard for. They provided freedom to serve, to live in silence, to tend to their faith within the acceptance of their own societies, their own cultures. And the results of their freedom empowered these women in a manner that is quite stunning and that ultimately created their own place in history.

We do not all choose to join an order of nuns, so how may we join a community united for a cause or passion and serve one another so selflessly? I think of the community of women who join forces in cities all across the country in solidarity to fight breast cancer. Women in all walks of life walk together for days to champion each other, in memory of those before them and to protect those who go behind them.

Service to one another does not only look like washing the bare feet of those who have given up their footwear. It also looks like a frozen casserole dish, a late-night phone call, a last-minute errand, and ultimately sacrifice for another.

A COMMUNITY OF CHANGE

Whether women's liberation was catapulted into being by Betty Friedan's work *The Feminine Mystique,* by the changes of a society burdened by economic demands beyond single breadwinner incomes, or by the improving landscape of career opportunities for women, its cause is debated. Most likely all these factors and more share responsibility, or credit, and by the early 1970s one hundred thousand women were members of consciousness-raising groups, some groups having formed as early as 1966.

These were commonly believed to be political activist groups, in part because the public introduction of the groups came at the first National Women's Liberation Conference in the late sixties. In truth, however, the consciousness-raising movement was not limited to the political arena. Nor was it tantamount to the feminist movement at the time. The publicly declared, official purpose of consciousness-raising groups was "to break down the barriers between women, encourage open communication among them, and help them develop pride in their sex."[2]

As had been the way of generations before them, women across America formed small groups of usually ten to twelve and commonly met in their homes.[3] It was here that they created safe communities to discuss what it meant to be a woman, to express frustrations, to support one another, and to strategize change. Only rather than meeting as gatherers whose husbands were away hunting, for bridge clubs or quilting guilds, these women came together to discuss their place in society, motherhood, their bodies, and the socially mandated image of beauty. They talked about sexuality and feelings of uselessness and disappointment as their gifts and interests went unused and unappreciated. The movement became a catalyst for change and is regarded as the largest support movement for women of its kind in this country.

Whatever your opinion about the feminist movement as a whole, its impact in bringing women together in honest community cannot be denied. Decades later, women who belonged to consciousness-raising groups speak of their circle of friends as diverse in race, socioeconomic status, and religion and distinguished by warmth, safety, love, support, and stability. Through their collective experiences, the women bolstered one another as they explored the issues in their lives that were personal to each one of them.

Sadly, as the societal change wrought by consciousness-raising groups opened the doors of unlimited opportunity for women, we walked through those doors and left behind the group dynamic of support. We became women alone once more as we competed with one another in the workplace, often cutting one another down, creating competition and jealousy among ourselves.

Rather than supporting one another in our endeavors, whether professional or otherwise, we compete, we overwork and stretch ourselves too thin, and we forget about our relationships or perhaps hope they will wait for us. This shift was what ultimately drove Lia Macko and Kerry Rubin to write *Midlife Crisis at 30* as a new generation of women reaped the effects of what began decades earlier and then sought again to bring change.

While we would not want to move backward in what women accomplished through consciousness-raising groups, I wish we could have held on to all that the women in those groups defined, including acceptance, safety, and, above all, uncompromising support. Today, a new generation of consciousness-raising groups could bring about revolutionary transformation in our communities of faith, friendships, and professions.

I suppose one notable characteristic of the consciousness-raising groups was authenticity. Women weren't pretending; rather they were grappling toward a new life and a new cultural landscape, and to make right what was wrong. Claiming to live a life that simply didn't exist would not accomplish what they wanted to achieve.

A COMMUNITY OF ACCEPTANCE

The lodge was set back from the road. Only a simple white sign with black street numbers, lit by a single spotlight, revealed its existence from the street. Outside the front doors of the old building, two women sat, seemingly unaware of the chilled air. One read from a notebook, "These are the people I need to make amends to…," while the other, older woman sitting opposite her listened intently, occasionally bringing a cigarette to her lips.

Just inside the door a counter supported a pan of home-made banana bread and a carafe of fresh coffee. Beyond the counter stretched a large room filled with dozens of people. There were women, men, teenagers. One man wore baggy sweatpants and an oversize sweatshirt with a baseball cap perched cockeyed on his head. Another man wore a blue dress shirt, edged with a white collar and cuffs, complete with cuff links and his initials embroidered on the sleeve. Seated in chairs all over the room, people took turns speaking their thoughts.

A tall, attractive, and large-framed man named Derek raised his hand. Wearing a buttery, caramel-colored leather coat, he shifted in his seat as he spoke. "This is my first time being here," he said. The room erupted in applause. "I had a really bad day," he continued. "But I had someone I could call, and I knew I could come here tonight and find understanding." He spoke of the network of support he was already receiving from people scattered about the large room. He spoke of problems with his ex-wife and about drinking too much—words that often beckon judgment from the hearts of others, but there was no judgment evident here. He spoke of his goals and his aspirations and thanked everyone for their friendship.

Sitting beside a little girl who looked to be three years old, a woman cradled a small baby in one arm and held a bottle to his mouth with her other hand. She spoke up, telling of how bad her day was, rife with busyness, chaos, and forgetfulness. Her daughter had an early morning appointment, but her husband had been up all night with the baby and was unable to help get her daughter ready. Later she had a doctor's appointment, and her baby, who was also sick, had a doctor's appointment as well. She spent the day in traffic, having forgotten her cell phone, running from here to there. And then as she neared her frustration limit, she was reminded of another perspective. Driving past a serious car accident, she realized her day was not that bad. This was life, and she was living it. And she was thankful.

She continued, thanking the others for their friendship. "The world is unsafe," she remarked. "The world is mean, but inside here there is a haven." She motioned to a man on another side of the room. "He helped me when I walked in and was struggling with my baby and my daughter." A lock of her dark hair streaked with blond highlights fell across her eye. Pushing it from her face, she finished, "The support that happens in here doesn't happen in the outside world." I saw Derek wipe tears from his face with the back of his hand.

A twenty-something with glasses spoke briefly of his struggle with accepting himself but also spoke of God's love for him, God's goodness, and the friendship of the people in the room. A woman in her thirties said she came tonight because she needed to feel loved and that she fought to love herself. The man beside her reached over and gave her shoulder a brotherly squeeze. Derek wiped his eyes once more.

Person after person piped up, all sharing from their hearts. Sometimes after an individual finished speaking, a few would echo, "Thanks for sharing." They all spoke of the friendship in the room and the acceptance they received from one another when they couldn't accept themselves. Some spoke of finally being able to find value in who they were, mistakes and all. One spoke of being humbled, another of her pride in what she had been able to accomplish because of the support of her friends there.

Each confession was peppered with simple wisdom that to me was profound. In speaking out of their experiences, they shared what they had discovered: the wisdom of a life lived with regret but also redemption.

Lastly, a woman stood and shared about her journey of faith in Jesus and her intimate relationship with him. "In my relationship with Jesus, I am filled with love. That love spreads so that I am able to love myself and then spills to a love of others." She spoke shyly, yet her voice rang with tones of humility and compassion. Before she took her seat again, another woman hugged her tightly and handed her a chip—a symbol of three years of sobriety. Everywhere around the room people clapped and cheered. And the Alcoholics Anonymous meeting concluded as the group formed a circle around the room, clasping hands, their voices uttering the Lord's Prayer.

I left the lodge in amazement. I had never seen anything like this group. In that room for an entire hour, there was no gender, no race, no age. There was no judgment, no expectation, and no self-righteousness. There was only acceptance and grace. The people in that room participated in one another's lives by supporting, listening, being available, empowering one another to be better, and loving one another even when they fell short of their own standards.

I found myself wondering, *Where else but here does a community characterized by such grace exist?* Sadly, most often we do not find that kind of friendship within our churches. We will not find it in our places of work, because, of course, work is largely about performance. And most of us do not find that complete acceptance even within our families.

Why do we have to know brokenness intimately to be able to show grace? In truth, we are all broken. So why are so few of our friendships characterized by complete acceptance? And how did the people in the lodge that evening know how to show love and friendship in a way I had never seen? They came there that night with no pretenses about who they were, what they wrestled with, and what they needed from each other. They were simply human.

The woman marking three years of sobriety gave this advice: "You have to work the steps with another person."

Speaking of the twelve steps, she said, "It's not enough to work the first three or four supported by someone and then think you can do it on your own. You have to work all twelve steps with someone else."

It was also a community of people who knew the power of friendship and how it empowered the individual as well. They weren't looking for codependency. They were already there because of dependency, and it had brought most of them to rock bottom. They were looking for support that would walk beside them along the way.

How can we have more friendships differentiated by such support, love, and acceptance as this? And before our friendships can be characterized by such an embrace, how can we first be people who are filled with love?

A COMMUNITY OF REFINEMENT

Communities dedicated to a cause, characterized by service, authenticity, and forgiveness—ultimately these communities exist to refine us. Says Carol Lee Flinders, "Life in an intentional community is like being inside one of those rotating cylinders full of water that rock collectors use to polish their rough treasures. Little by little, over the years, a lot of the roughest edges get smoothed away. Maybe we even begin to shine a bit."[4]

Living life alongside someone else, cohabiting in joy, disappointment, accomplishment, or betrayal—this kind of living is not relegated to a convent, an AA meeting, or a club gathering. But choosing to engage in community, to continually and consistently open our lives to others and allow them to peek inside, to listen, and perhaps to speak or stand in silent solidarity can only change us. Perhaps it softens our sharper corners, perhaps it invites contemplation and thought, perhaps we choose to act as a result, but we cannot emerge from community unchanged if we enter with great awareness and intentionality. Those rough edges are buffed to a shine then reflect what is inside. And isn't that the very gift of community?

But of course we are not always able to plug into a community in the way we would like. So is it possible to bring these traits of community friendship into our relationships? Anne Morrow Lindbergh wrote of the responsibilities of women, and especially American women, in the pace of life we've adopted. With all that encompasses life as we know it, how can one give attention to all the aspects of life we desire? Many lives are filled by overscheduled calendars, the management of a household, responsibility in the care of children, spouses, a career, and the resulting social obligations all three require, not to mention desiring further time to give attention to friends, other family members, body and spiritual wellness.

Writes Lindbergh, "I cannot shed my responsibilities. I cannot permanently inhabit a desert island. I cannot be a nun in the midst of family life."[5] And most of us wouldn't want to anyway. But we can glean treasures from what we witness and experience, giving them over into the areas of our lives that may be enriched by these treasures.

I've sat on the beach many times and with amusement observed children building sandcastles. They grab their buckets and hurtle themselves down to the ocean to fill them with water, the element much needed to build or refresh their castles. Then, treasure in hand, they run with the same urgency back to their castles, using the gift from the sea as they deem fit. One of the aspects of this activity I find so amusing is the speed and intensity with which the task is done. There is no sauntering, no hesitation. No, it is down to the water at mach speed and then back again to engage in castle building as if time is of the essence. Perhaps in their childish wisdom, they know better than we that, as it is with sandcastles, the opportunity to build life's relationships will not last forever. What, then, are we waiting for?

This act of bringing home treasure is what Lindbergh did when she wrote her book *Gift from the Sea*. Using what she observed in her solitude by the sea, she brought wisdom into the other areas of her life. How do we serve our friends, our sisters, so completely? How do we love one another without judgment and with acceptance? How do we empower one another to live more fully into the women we were created to be? What can we learn from these communities that we can bring back as gifts to enrich our own friendships and our own communities as we know them?

ELEVEN

Circle of Friends

As soon as I entered the coffee shop, I was greeted by warmth. Symbols of the season alerted me that the holidays were upon us: snowflakes, Christmas trees, color schemes in shades of red and green for Christmas and blue and silver for Hanukkah, stocking stuffers, gift ideas. Christmas music wafted through the air, and the gingerbread latte was back—in the red cups! I thrilled inwardly at the nostalgia of the season, feeling pangs of gratefulness to be alive.

And as I looked around that Saturday morning, I saw groups of women scattered throughout the shop. Most were casual in sweats or workout clothes, while sweatshirts and jackets on others announced the cold weather. They were clustered together, too many chairs clumped around the tiny two-person tables. They laughed, caught up on the week's events with one another, and sipped slowly. I watched them, waiting for my name to be called to announce the arrival of my beverage, with way too many descriptors that would prove my ability to have my drink just the way I like it. And I felt a twinge of envy. I thought of my girlfriends and wished for time together with them that morning, sitting in Starbucks, enjoying one another's company. I stepped back into the chilly morning but was warmed by what my senses had taken in, the memories the visit had invoked, the community I felt part of.

There are the Steel Magnolias, the Ya-Ya Sisters, and the Sisterhood of the Traveling Pants, to name a few—famous groups of girlfriends that reflect the friendships we all long for. Girl power, a pink wedding, sworn sisterhood, and a summer of magic—I loved them all.

And there were another four famous friends I got to know really well: Charlotte, Samantha, Miranda, and Carrie. For six seasons and ninety-four episodes, I experienced vicariously through the four friends the search for Mr. Right, bad dates, cosmetic procedures gone awry, marriages, divorce, pregnancy, infertility, professional success, and all the trendiest New York City restaurants—without any of the calories.

One particular New Year's Eve, I sat fully engrossed in a *Sex and the City* all-night marathon. Yes, it was the shoes, the longing, and the romance, but mostly it was the friendships that captured me. I was quite content to kick off my shoes for an evening and step into Carrie's and into her circle of friends.

Hers were the kinds of friends who have time for you whenever you need them, who cheer you on, who listen to your every question, your every neurosis without judging—or rarely anyway. And in Carrie's world, if you should have a little spat with one of your friends, it's easily resolved in thirty minutes or less without the wounded residue that sticks to you both for a while in real-world, postargument friendships.

So there I sat at three o'clock in the morning. Having nearly forgotten the presence of a male companion who was also watching from the nearby sofa, I was curled up in an overstuffed milk chocolate–colored leather chair that felt brand-new, though it was not, simply because it had been temporarily moved to another part of the living room to make room for the lighted Christmas tree that still held its place of honor. I had changed out of my black velvet pants and sequined tee from earlier New Year's revelry and was now in my pj's. And suddenly, interrupting a fabulous fashion moment that included both Dolce and Gabbana and Heidi Klum, the male voice remarked, "That could never happen."

"What could never happen?" I responded, only half listening because Carrie's falling facedown on a fashion runway held most of my attention.

"*That*. Their friendship. Four girls could never have as seamless a friendship as they portray. Women are too jealous and competitive to all be such good friends like that."

"That's not true," I immediately protested and crossed

my arms, prepared to defend my gender as the owner of the comment cast a shadow over the hours I'd been basking in the pink glow emanating from couture, Manolos, and kindred estrogen. "Well, it could happen…," I trailed off weakly, not able to muster up much gusto to argue a point I was going to lose in the end anyway. I knew he'd go for the winning jab by bringing up my own previous experiences as a participant in group friendships.

And it was true: on more than one occasion, he sat and listened to my complaining, lamenting, and even bitter diatribes and tears over group friendships that later dissolved. Not that my friendships with all the individuals involved had entirely ended, but the group friendships in my previous experiences had suffered an acrimonious demise, mostly due to the prolonged rub of jealousy, competition, guilt, and oversensitivity. Eventually there was a big and raw gaping hole, and so we went our separate ways.

I had to admit that to an extent he had a point, at least based on my own experiences to date. What is it about getting a group of women together that brings out our competitive nature, jealousy, envy, and gossiping tendencies? Why do we purr contentedly over our relationships one day, then claw our friends in cattiness another? Are four friendships as portrayed in *Sex and the City* that out of the question?

Okay, I know they are not real. I realize it's only television. Plenty of other clues reveal the implausibility of it all: they seem to have bottomless checkbooks, impossibly fast metabolisms, and unusually large Manhattan apartments, and they escape the majority of their escapades with the opposite sex unscathed, both body and soul. But their practice of friendship bears looking at just the same. Do Miranda, Charlotte, and Samantha hate Carrie because she eats whatever she wants and maintains a size zero and a six pack? Do they talk bad about her behind her back, labeling her with crass names because she wears clothes that reveal her bra? Were the other girls jealous when Miranda made partner at her firm or Carrie scored a book deal? Do they covet one another's clothes, shoes, bags, and hair? Does one flirt with another's boyfriend? No, they don't. Yet many real-life friendships among women are plagued with those very same feelings and scenarios.

One inconsequential Monday evening gave me pause to think about such friendships. I was working retail in a women's boutique on a slow night. Perhaps because they spent too much on Saturday and Sunday, no customers were in the store, and so I decided to try on a pair of red, bootcut corduroys I'd had my eye on. After slipping into them, I padded barefoot out of the dressing room and stood in front of an enormous mirror to get a better look. Balancing on my tiptoes, I checked out my reflection at every angle. My coworker, a male, stood by and lent his opinion.

"I think they're too tight on my rear end," I lamented, partly to myself, standing with my back to the mirror and craning my neck around to get a better look at my behind.

"No, they're not," he insisted. "That's how they're supposed to fit." He continued, "You only say that because you're used to shopping with women. Women always tell each other that things are too tight when they shop together. They're envious when their friends look good, and they tell them things look good when they don't."

I didn't know if I agreed with him or not, but I did buy the pants. That thought had never occurred to me before. I had never even considered telling another friend she looked good in something when she didn't, nor had I worried someone would do the same to me. But I was intrigued that my coworker had that unfavorable impression of female friendships.

Is the bad rap fair? Are we as women sometimes so jealous of each other that we are dishonest and manipulative? In the deepest recesses of our hearts, do we not always want the best, do we not want happiness and success, for our friends? Sadly, too often it seems that we do not.

Then why open yourself up to the cattiness, the jealousy, the competition that fester in group friendships? For whether you are the giver or receiver of such behavior, neither feels good. So why do we do it? Why do we form groups of friends? We celebrate birthdays together; we take trips; we read books or develop hobbies with our group.

These groups differ from the collective community groups. Bringing the collective smaller and closer to the individual, these groups are usually three to four in number. And rather than being brought together by common interests or commitments, shared pasts, brokenness, or goals, these groups come together because of a real kindredness, a joining of souls and hearts, and often in spite of circumstances rather than because of them.

Regardless of age we form little cliques like we did when we were in school. We sometimes even give our groups nicknames like the Saving Graces, the Steel Magnolias, or the Georgia Peaches, to name a few I've heard (obviously I live in the south). And much like a family, we take on roles. There's the organizer, the mother of the group. There's the one we all wish we could be like; she seems to have it all. There's the one who likes to be mothered and cared for or who doesn't quite have it together but is content that way. There's the member who just wants to make sure everyone is happy. There's the one you go to for advice, the one you go to for comfort, the one you go to for a laugh. Then we build alliances; we discuss with one member of the group how another has annoyed us or hurt our feelings. Sometimes we cast judgment on one person's choices with a couple of others. Or we compare the treatment each group member gets. We discuss who was called first to be invited on an outing or, more important, who was called last, and then the unforgivable, who was not called at all. And then we come back together as one big happy family. We're close again, and all is right with the world.

So why all the jealousy and competition? Why can't we just get on with the coming together part? There is a peculiar dynamic created by groups of friends. To begin, we size ourselves up against our friends, and group friendships provide a collection of measuring units for all sorts of categories—weight, muscle tone, fashion sense, happy romantic relationships, well-adjusted children, talent; the list goes on. As Virginia Woolf said in *The Waves,* "We use our friends to measure our own stature."[1] And so our acceptance of ourselves is based on how we measure up against whatever standard we have set, as though two or more people can't wear the same crown. And no one wants to be the first runner-up or just the nominee. Sure, it's an honor just to be nominated, but who doesn't want to actually go home with the award?

And perhaps it's not only about winning. Perhaps it's actually our awareness of our connection with these friends and our desire to be in relationship with them that makes all the stakes higher. As women, our awareness of feelings, responsibility, and community is heightened. Could it be this heightened awareness increases our tendency to nurse hurt feelings, to feel slighted or pushed away?

The truth is that for all the idiosyncrasies we find in groups of friends, we find wholeness there too. We bring different people together who contribute their gifts, their wisdom, and their personalities. We know who to cry with, talk politics with, gossip with about celebrities, or take shopping. But collectively we bring a fully thinking, feeling, and sometimes laughing body together. A collected group of true friends gives awareness to the individuals, bearing witness and bringing significance to our identities and our journeys, lest we remain lost in a larger world.

Music artist Brandi Carlile sings about the stories of who she is and where she's been but then pauses to ask, "What good are the stories if there is no one to hear them?" Our small community of friends gives honor to the stories that are ours to tell.

Carol Gilligan has explored the psychological development and behavior of women, as compared to men, in relationships. Conducting a test among male and female college students, Gilligan, along with Susan Pollack, set out to study the differences in interpretations of violence between the sexes and how issues of separation and connection are central to their perceptions of violence.

To conduct the test, the researchers presented six pictures to the students and asked them to write stories in response to the visual images. Two of the pictures showed a man and woman in close affiliation: a man and woman sitting by the river, and two trapeze artists gripping each other by the wrists. The man's bent knees hung over the trapeze bar, but the woman hung in midair, anchored only to the man. Two other pictures showed people in impersonal achievement situations: a man sitting at his desk in a high-rise office building, and two women in lab coats working in a laboratory. It's remarkable to note that the men perceived violence and aggression in the interpersonal scenes rather than the impersonal achievement images, while the women responded vice versa. In other words, while men associated danger with circumstances of intimacy, women identified danger in scenes of isolation, a fear of standing out or being left alone. Ultimately the danger for men was in connection; the danger for women was in isolation.

But something else in the study jumped out at me. When writing stories about the trapeze artists, 22 percent of the women added nets in their stories about the acrobats, though no net was shown in the picture. Only 6 percent of the men did this, while 40 percent of the men mentioned that there was no net and that this could mean certain death for the acrobats. While the men perceived violence in the death of the trapeze artists, a high number of the women made the scene safer by their addition of nets that would protect the acrobats, thereby saving their lives. Says Gilligan, "As women imagine the activities through which relationships are woven and connection sustained, the world of intimacy—which appears so mysterious and dangerous to men—comes instead to appear increasingly coherent and safe."[2]

That is what our friendship groups are. They are our

safety nets. Because sometimes you fall so hard that you need more than one person to catch you. Because somehow in the end, after all the conflict and cattiness, it all smoothes out, and we remember why we love these other women.

A friend of mine from college e-mailed me excitedly to report on her experience during a girls' weekend with old friends. A group of women she had been friends with gathered at the mountain home of the woman who coerced them into a reunion. When the time came for the trip, my friend regretted her acceptance of the invitation and was certain the weekend would be awkward and strained while they all got reacquainted and caught up. Instead, she reported great openness and, ultimately, healing among the women as they shared candidly the disappointments and regrets, the setbacks and joys of the last years. My friend returned home buoyed and rejuvenated by these girlfriends from years ago, fortified by both the strength of where they'd once been and where they were today, as well as the authenticity with which they celebrated their journeys.

While I was writing this chapter, I shared my thoughts about it with a friend. "I don't have groups of friends now," she confided. "I used to, but it's too hard."

"It's complicated," I agreed, sympathizing with her past hurt that all of a sudden seemed close to the surface. "But somehow I still have hope," I continued. "I still think groups of friends can be really wonderful, in spite of the complications."

"You should write that," she said.

"What?" I queried.

"That," she said. "Write that you have hope."

Perhaps because group friendships, by nature, can be complicated and need just the right chemistry—they can't be forced—we often don't seek those groups out. Instead we simply discover that we are in one, whether by circumstance, geography, or commonalities. That has been my experience the past few years.

Somehow I found myself in a new group of friends. I awakened to this belonging about a year ago when I introduced a guy I was sort of seeing to my group of girlfriends. My sister moved that day, and without even a thought we all came out to help, boyfriends and husbands in tow. It was a September Saturday and pouring rain, and we had an assortment of SUVs, four-door sedans, a single pickup truck, and a small U-Haul van. Finally, wet and tired, the move completed, we congregated at a neighborhood pizza place for dinner.

There I sat, grubby and famished, at a table full of my friends while we ordered more pizza and pitchers of drinks than our hungry eyes could consume. For a moment I mentally stepped back, trying to visualize what my new friend was glimpsing as he became acquainted with these who were dear to me. As I watched the laughing faces, took in the conversation, and tried to make sense of what was being said with everyone talking at once, it occurred to me that I had everything I needed in that moment. I was safe. Right then, I felt perfectly content.

Maybe we find ourselves in a community of girlfriends, whether we intended to write the story that way or not, because we see the need for a net and for intentional community. In the presence of a net of girlfriends, we find support, silliness, frustration, disappointment, laughter, affection, shared thoughts and experiences, danger, refinement, and yet safety. Because a group of girlfriends is just that. With all the relationship risks, flips, thrills, and misses, they catch us whether we feel we need it right then or not. And because even if we don't, eventually we will.

TWELVE

The Spaces Between Us

I don't know what caused her to seem to slip away,
what invited her to that place where she did not engage
those around her. But I always suspected it was when
disappointments became too much and buried her.

I had my own share of disappointments. That
spring, though new life was evidenced as barren
branches grew leaves, buds became flowers, and the
bitterness of cold was chased away, I could not bring
myself to new life inside. I felt desperate for the support
of my friends. I had no strength of my own left and was
in earnest need of borrowing strength from someone
else. Only no one seemed to have any to spare.

She and I would go out and talk, but there was a
wall between us. I'd broach the subject, and she'd only

go so far. She didn't ask much; perhaps she was afraid to probe, afraid she would be invading my privacy. But I needed her to. There was too much in my head to sift through what I wanted to tell. I needed it to just spill out, but first I needed someone to remove the lid. But she stuck to what I volunteered or thought to say. And in truth she never said much in response. Maybe it was all too close to home for her. I don't know, and I never asked. I wanted more from her, needed more. She didn't seem to have it to give or at least didn't offer it.

Sometimes I think she retreats when she feels fulfilled in other areas of her life. And sometimes I think she goes away because her untold disappointment with life is too deep. Is it space she needs, or does she need to be coaxed out? How do I reach her? How do I be her friend when I don't know what she wants? And how do I say what I need too?

Then the ice thawed, and she opened again. But I could not respond.

Whether it was because of the nostalgia the holiday season brings or because of traditions that seem to neither acknowledge nor pay tribute to what has changed during the year, my own problems seemed even greater to me. The hurt they caused was so palpable I could no longer even speak of it. Whereas before then I needed my friends, needed them to be involved in the journey

I was on, now I only wanted space. I stopped asking, stopped talking, stopped trying to get what I needed. I retreated inside to lick my wounds and feel sorry for myself. I pitied myself in my emotional aloneness and in my disappointments. I was ready to write them off, write all of them off, and maybe I actually did a little.

Then in passing, another friend remarked to me that it had been a hard year for all of us. It was true. The year had been filled with setbacks and disappointments for the whole lot of us. Honestly, I'd never considered that. I was too lost in my own mire. And maybe because my own struggles were more visible, more in my face, I had been blinded by them as they obstructed my vision of others. Or perhaps because they were so enormous to me, I assumed they looked the same size to everyone. I'd forgotten that often when the mirror you're looking in is your own, objects may be closer than they appear to others. Now it was my turn to thaw. I warmed to them all once more.

Looking back, as I trace the years of our friendship, I see a rhythm to her and to us. We drift apart at times, and the friendship seems stilted, sometimes forced. And then we're together again with much laughter, deep conversations, and shared opinions and passions, and we have a long run. Sometimes I think I like her more than she likes me, and sometimes I wonder if

🌱 she believes the same. Sometimes I wonder if we'll always be friends, and sometimes I can't imagine we'll never be.

In every friendship, no matter how close, we inevitably feel the spaces between us. The unspoken words, the hurts we don't share because we weren't asked or because no one was listening, the perceived slights we don't express—these fill that empty space and make it grow wider, ballooning between us, pushing us farther apart. The expanding space has the potential to explode, permanently injuring those in its path, and it can be lethal to relationships. What do we do with that space? Do we talk about it? Do we force the air out of it? Do we let it run its course?

There is another type of space between us. It is the space we need to save ourselves or even to preserve our relationship. Interestingly enough, one of the original Hebrew words used to indicate "salvation" is also used to mean "space." And there are times when that space can save us. Space can give us perspective, time to breathe, time to listen. My favorite poet, William Butler Yeats, writes,

Come near, come near, come near—Ah, leave me still
A little space for the rose-breath to fill![1]

How do you give space to a friendship without letting it drift away? Space, like silence, makes us uncomfortable sometimes. We don't know what to do with quiet, emptiness, and loss. And all of those things create space. But space allows us to grow, and without it we are stifled, our growth stunted. When we grieve we want to rush to feel better so that we don't continue to hurt, rather than allow space for that grieving. And when things aren't right with another person we care about, we often rush to fill the space, forcing things to surface that are not yet ready.

Living things need space to transform. I learned this little truth quite literally. I've never had much of a green thumb, but I love the beauty of flowers, so I keep trying to bring them into my space. One Saturday afternoon while trolling a nursery in search of opportunities to capture beauty, I purchased some potted pink tulips, some of my most favorite flowers. Upon bringing them home I noticed the decorative ceramic pot I intended to put them in was too small. No matter. I lifted them gingerly from the generic plastic bucket I'd brought them home in and promptly shoved them into the tiny blue and white ceramic planter I'd painted myself. I discarded the excess soil that I couldn't pack into the overflowing planter and drizzled some water into the soil, now tight and compact, my transplant complete.

They were dead in a week. The reason is simple; they

didn't have enough space. Similarly, we fill what little space we have with sounds, objects, and distractions, cramming the space full, leaving no room for mystery, patience, or growth.

So how do we give our friendships what they sometimes need? Space is sitting with your friend in silence, space is allowing her to find her way in her time, space is sometimes suspending judgment, space is not always needing to have the right words or the right advice, and space can be simply walking away for a time, even just to stand a short distance away.

And how do we know what a friend requires? Let's be honest: we play games sometimes. I don't know if men do this, but I know women will at times push others away or choose not to respond to their overtures, not because they want to be left alone, but because they want someone to try harder, to hunt them down and say literally, "I am *here* for you." Other times we need the space, want it, but we just don't know how to ask for it. Men would roll their eyes at this contradiction and ask how they are supposed to know what it is we really want.

Sometimes we don't know what our friend wants, even when we've known her through many of life's seasons. Sometimes we don't even know what we want for ourselves. And sometimes when we get what we need, we find we don't need it anymore. And anyway, even if we do know what to do for our friend at one time, it may not be that way the next time.

The point is we can never stop paying attention. A friend once asked me if I thought our mutual friend needed space or presence with what she was going through. It was a good question, and I responded truthfully that I just didn't know but that I was trying both.

Even when we truly want to do the right thing by our friends, we sometimes just don't know. And so we persevere. We learn sometimes by pushing too hard and sometimes by giving too much space. And if we are the ones who are given too much space, more than we wanted, when we feel let down, as though others weren't there for us, what then? The fact is sometimes we are let down by our friends. Intentions may be good, efforts misguided, or they may have nothing left to give, and the result is simply that they are unable to be there for us in the ways we expect them to be.

What I have learned from my own experience is simply this: there are times in friendship—perhaps even in every relationship—when we need to simply accept what people are able to give. That is part of being a friend; in fact, that is part of living among others in any type of community. It is necessary to put away the expectations, the goals, the fixing and longing for how it could be, and simply be and allow our friend to do the same.

In her treasured work *Gift from the Sea,* Anne Morrow Lindbergh writes, "Security in a relationship lies neither in looking back to what it was in nostalgia, nor forward to what it might be in dread or anticipation, but living in the present relationship and accepting it as it is now. For relationships, too, must be like islands. One must accept them for what they are here and now, within their limits."[2]

THIRTEEN

Companions Along
the Journey

She used to be my friend. And I don't know why she no longer is.

I first met her when I worked for her. My husband was in law school, and I was working two jobs—my full-time job and a part-time job at a women's retail store that afforded me the opportunity to buy clothes even with our tight budget. She resigned her manager's position a few months after I started, and I heard through other co-workers that she got engaged and eventually married.

A year or more later, my husband and I ran into them both at a church small-group thing. It was one of those evenings every introvert hates. About seventy-five twenty- and thirty-somethings descended onto someone's home in the suburbs in the hopes of getting connected to a small group. We didn't know a soul, and thankfully neither did they. As my husband and I wound our way through a sea of unfamiliar faces, I spotted hers and made a beeline. We spent the evening talking with them—or rather I shadowed them everywhere they went, determined not to lose the small triumph of the one connection we'd made. It only made sense then that we'd join the same small group.

Our friendship with them progressed, and before long we were meeting for dinner regularly on weekends and even vacationed together a few times. It's hard to find couple friends, two people both of you like. They were the only couple we'd met that we both enjoyed spending time with. And she and I began to do things together without the guys as well. We shopped together, talked on the phone, and eventually stepped gingerly into the waters of authenticity with each other—at least we waded into the shallow end. But it was a lot for me at the time, and I got the same sense from her. She didn't get too honest too easily.

We went to dinner one night, the four of us, and I noticed she was quiet most of the evening. The next day I called her and asked if she was okay. She said she was fine but didn't give too much other insight into her mood. I let it go but still wondered if something was wrong. Several weeks later she e-mailed me to tell me she was pregnant. Around the same time I got my first book contract, and I became busy working on the manuscript and traveling on weekends for research. We didn't keep in touch much during that time. I didn't see her for seven months, and then I got an invitation to her baby shower. When she saw me, she told me I was too skinny, I told her she was adorable—and she was. Her petite frame had retained its smallness, all but the seeming impossibly large belly that still had a month to go.

I didn't see her again until about a year later when I ran into her in a sandwich shop. I missed her, though, and wondered what happened. How did we just stop being friends? Was it the baby? Did she think I couldn't relate? Was it my busyness with my book? Did I inadvertently offend her?

Another year passed, and then I found myself making awkward small talk with her outside Barnes and Noble. We exchanged the obligatory, "How are you?" and were about to falter into clumsy conversation when her little boy, perhaps sensing that we needed help, rescued us from ourselves and piped up in two-year-old baby talk, "I'm getting a new stroller!" Bless that child!

I asked him a series of questions, and, thankfully, not only did he understand me, but I, too, deciphered every answer he gave. I asked about her burgeoning belly, the usual questions: gender, due date. She didn't ask much of me, which made it obvious she'd heard of my divorce. And then we wrapped up the conversation without too much unease and said our good-byes.

We didn't make empty promises to call or suggest getting together, parting words that usually seem obligatory when you run into an old friend. No, it seemed clear it was over between us and we'd theoretically moved on. But I didn't want it to be over. I felt sad the rest of the day, wondering why she stopped liking me.

What happens with the friendships that escape us? How does it happen that you drift apart, one day waking up to realize you're no longer friends with that person anymore? Nothing was said; there was no fight, no apparent offense. You don't call her, she doesn't call you, and she simply becomes the friend who got away. Perhaps it is circumstances—someone's situation changes.

When catching up on the phone with an old friend, I asked how a close friend of hers, whom I also knew peripherally, was faring. "We're not really friends anymore," she said. I expressed surprise; when I had visited her a few years earlier, the two were tight. "Well, I have a baby, and she doesn't," was her matter-of-fact response. To which I could only summon an, "Oh," in response.

But it's true: marriage, babies, singleness, divorce, and even success are all life circumstances that can grow into the spaces between friends and push the friends further from each other. Other times friendships are born out of geographical convenience. It then becomes difficult to maintain a friendship when one has moved away. Sadly our lives become so full it is often difficult to maintain that relationship when distance crosses between two people. Some friendships are created out of immediate commonality, and when shared circumstances change, the friendship fades too.

And perhaps there are those who enter our lives only for a time. They bring purpose, experience, and companionship that is meant to last only for a season. Perhaps we always knew that would be the case. Or perhaps we thought it was something we could hold on to and maintain despite our differences or circumstance. Whatever we once thought, much like the magical Mary Poppins, when the winds change, she is gone.

It was December, and I was headed on a research trip to India that meant missing holiday parties, shopping, and Christmas carols. When I returned, it would be the day

before Christmas Eve. I was a writer for hire, con-
tracted to ghostwrite a book, and I was traveling to
India to experience the story firsthand. My travel com-
panions were about twenty students majoring in communication and in search of documentary
opportunities.

I stood in the Atlanta airport, waiting to depart,
negotiating the sale of my home on my BlackBerry.
When I returned I would have two weeks to find a
place to live, pack up my house, and move into a new
place. And I had just found out that the main target of
my research would not be meeting me in India. This
was not good news. The timing of the trip was poor,
scheduled only to accommodate college vacation sched-
ules, and now it seemed my trip would be pointless.

There I stood in Hartsfield-Jackson Atlanta International Airport, clutching my passport and tapping
my tennis-shoed toe in agitation, my mood darkening
by the second. Then I heard our group leaders call out
roommates. A two-week tour of three-star hotels in
southern India with a perfect stranger. I was too long
out of college for this to be good news.

Professionally, the trip would prove to be an utter
waste of my time. It turned out that traveling with the
group didn't really work for the purposes of my research,
as the others had separate agendas and, therefore, needs

that differed from mine. But I will be forever thankful it all constellated that way, because over those two weeks, I became true friends with my roommate.

She was a beauty queen from South Carolina, statuesque and gracious. Life had sucker-punched her a few times, but her faith was simple, strong, and so very real. Her love for God practically dripped from her pores. But it was the real thing. She talked about God and her faith all the time, but it wasn't put on; it was completely genuine. And her simple steadfast faith cut through the shell of my cynicism. I'd been in Christian ministry a long time, and I'd come to doubt—not God but people, and specifically some of God's people.

My life was tumbling down around me then, not looking even a little bit the way I'd dreamed it would. I'd been crying out to God for years over circumstances far beyond my control, and I felt I'd received nothing. No change, no answers, no peace. I spoke of much, but I stopped short of telling her all that, though I'm sure she sensed some of these things, as women do. As much as the love of God poured from her, I'm sure wounded faith and disappointment were oozing from me. But I mostly listened to her. I asked her questions too. When she spoke of doing what God called her to do, I asked her how she knew. It was a genuine question to a person I believed was genuine. And so I really wanted to know. I listened as she talked about her life and God's faithfulness to her and to those she loved.

We became inseparable those two weeks. We ate all our meals together, saw the sun rise on the southern tip of India, crashed a wedding party, and processed together all we were seeing and how it was changing us. By the end of the trip, we were staying up all night talking. When we stopped in Paris on the route home, we climbed to the top of the Eiffel Tower to glimpse the rose-hued city in the morning sun. We talked a few times after returning home. She became engaged to her boyfriend, a pastor, and five months later I drove the two hours to attend her wedding. Alone, I stayed at the reception just long enough to say hello, hug her, and grab a cupcake for the road home.

I talked to her only once after that. I think of her often, though, with warmth and appreciation. Nothing in my circumstances changed on that trip. But I did. For fourteen days I stepped out of the shadows and warmed myself in the glow of faith seen in others. And she was one of them. I guess that's all it was intended to be.

What do we do with the friend who got away? Do we pursue her, hunt her down, refuse to let her escape? When I saw one friendship was slipping away, I didn't try to stop it. I didn't ask why; I didn't take the time to ask if I offended her or hurt her feelings in some way. I simply let it go, licking my wounds of rejection. And now it seems like too much time has passed, so there is no explanation. But perhaps even if I had asked, there would have been no explanation. Perhaps she just needed to get away.

What if a friend for whatever reason needs the distance? How do we know when to let her go, when to pursue? How do we not give up too easily and yet respect a friend's need to let go?

❦ We were the best of friends. I never held back my feelings or thoughts; I told her everything. We'd meet for lunch when I could knock off of work for a short while or grab coffee on late Saturday mornings. With my kids planted happily in front of Cartoon Network and my husband trimming the hedges that grow under the front windows of the house, I'd escape for a few hours, and we'd catch up on the last several days over foamy and artificially flavored lattes.

We walked through some impossibly painful times together: deaths of family members, illnesses, rebellious children. I was there for her as much as I knew how, and I thought it was enough. She, too, was there for me.

And then she started spending time with someone else. She told me about her new friend, but I never picked up that a confession of a new friend was just that—a confession that she would no longer be mine. And strangely, surprisingly, she faded out of my life. I went to her and asked what had happened, whether I had done anything to hurt her. She denied that anything was wrong or even different. She simply never shared in my life again the way she had. Gone were the two-hour lunches and Saturday morning coffees. No more quick phone calls in the middle of the day when one of us had something we just had to tell.

I still see her, and when I do I feel jealousy. I feel jealousy when I glimpse her laughing and talking with friends at the coffee shop where we used to meet. I feel envy when the small group she leads at our church is larger and seems more popular than the group I lead. And I feel resentful of the closeness with friends she seems to still have in her life, when I have not been able to discover another friendship like the one we shared together.

Recovering from the breakup of a friendship requires healing. To be friends necessitates trust, honesty, and—the hardest of all—vulnerability. It is easy to feel like friendships that get away snatch a piece of us with them. But they leave something with us too. More than disappointment, hurt, or wounds, they leave the experiences of shared emotions, events, conversations, and wisdom folded into the creases in our lives, enriching them with texture. These creases in our souls become the lines that groove our faces. We see lines of laughter, lines of sadness, and lines of deep thought, and they become a part of the story our lives tell.

Stanzas from a beautiful yet sad poem by Henry Wadsworth Longfellow sing with wistfulness of the friend who got away.

We sat within the farm-house old,
    Whose windows, looking o'er the bay,
Gave to the sea-breeze damp and cold,
    An easy entrance, night and day.

Not far away we saw the port,
    The strange, old-fashioned, silent town,
The lighthouse, the dismantled fort,
    The wooden houses, quaint and brown.

We sat and talked until the night,
    Descending, filled the little room;
Our faces faded from the sight,
    Our voices only broke the gloom.

We spake of many a vanished scene,
    Of what we once had thought and said,
Of what had been, and might have been,
    And who was changed, and who was dead;

And all that fills the hearts of friends,
    When first they feel, with secret pain,
Their lives thenceforth have separate ends,
    And never can be one again.[1]

There is no doubt that certain friends leave an indelible mark on us, for good or for bad. They bring so much to our lives, and then we move on without them. It is never easy to simply let go, even when we are being asked to, as friendships sometimes do.

But then there are friends we release. They did not simply and inexplicably escape us; rather we sent them away. What about the friendships we choose to leave behind?

When we fell into the step of friendship, she confided to me, "No one stays my friend." She tucked her dark hair behind her ear. "I'm too much. In the end they always leave me."

It was spoken like a challenge, a call to be different from everyone who had let her down. And inwardly I was sure I'd be different. For this woman, whose life had so far been defined by rejection, disappointment, and indifference, I was prepared to be an unconditional friend, and I was certain I had both the patience and the tenacity to commit to this friendship.

I supported her in all the ways we express friendship: listening, offering advice, celebrating triumphs, mourning disappointments, and rescuing her when she needed it. When people cast criticism her way, I hotly defended her. In spite of patterns I'd begun to recognize, I clutched tightly to my belief in her and to my commitment to friendship. I rooted for her, championed her, and ultimately thought I could save her— even from herself. But she did not want to be saved.

And I began to realize that rather than rescuing her, I was making her comfortable. She was sleeping in the bed she had made for herself, and I was tucking her in and wishing her sweet dreams.

In one last effort to inspire her to step onto the life raft I'd provided, I gave her an ultimatum. I dangled our friendship in front of her, but regrettably she didn't bite. She said she couldn't, wasn't ready, and so I drifted away from her. I did what I never wanted to do. I increased her rejection statistic. Now I, too, would be among the motley crew who had left her. I would be part of the story she'd tell another friend one day. But

even with the bitter taste of that reality and knowing
I had disappointed her like so many others before me,
I knew I had chosen the only answer I could. I could
not help her, nor could I save her. And in the end I
could not be her friend. To do so would only pull
her further down, perhaps bringing me along in the
undertow.

What about the friendships we consciously end? George
Eliot said with frankness, "Friendships begin with liking or
gratitude—roots that can be pulled up."[2] Certainly friendships, like every relationship, have ups and downs. Any relationship that has the capacity to bring much laughter, joy,
and strength springs from cells of humanity. This humanity
holds the potential for pain, jealousy, ill-intentions, wrong-
doing, stubbornness, and manipulation, but also great resiliency and grace.

So when do we decide one particular relationship must
end? How do we determine when a relationship requires a
death or end because it demands more than we want to give
or feel we are able to give? How do we know the difference
between what is life giving and what is suffocating our very
breath? It would seem that we would easily know the difference, but are we always that intentional in our friendships to
choose only what is life giving? We will often choose a rela-

tionship that drains us for a variety of reasons, some conscious, some not. Some choices come from a martyr complex; others come from a guilt complex. Some people merely fear the small but powerful word *no*.

Does ending a friendship feel like a refusal to forgive or like an act of selfishness? Do we feel that to love can look only one way or means we always make the same choice? What if the very act of ending is also an act of love toward either ourselves or another?

Rosalind Wiseman prescribes a bill of rights for friendships in her bestseller *Queen Bees and Wannabes*. Prompting a girl to consider such questions as, "What does she want and need in a friendship?" "What are her rights and responsibilities in a friendship?" and, "What are her friends' rights and responsibilities in the friendship?"[3] the bill provides a list of standards intended to guide adolescent girls as they navigate the murky and often stormy waters of friendship.

I was in the eighth grade when my mother found a note from one of my best girlfriends. I had hurriedly emptied out my backpack, leaving a messy pile of tests, handouts, notebooks, and a folded note atop my dresser. The note contained talk of activities I was not permitted to engage in and language I was not permitted to use. But there was a third strike against the note. Someone had evidently found the note and added unkind comments in the margins of the wide-ruled notebook paper. I had actually not even seen this, as the prank (which smacked of thirteen-year-old boys) had been pulled after I had already read the note and tucked it into my backpack to discard later.

But to my mom it looked like my friend had written me a mean note. Probably in a moment of parental panic, my mother told me I had to end my friendship with the author of the note. I begged for the decision to be overturned. I tried without success to convince my mother that I didn't speak that way (not entirely true), that I was not influenced by my friends (completely not true), and that my friend was not mean to me at all and never had been (that part was actually true). But in my mother's effort to instill in me convictions and conduct becoming of a Christian and a young lady and my own bill of rights for friendships, she insisted I end the friendship.

I still remember my friend Jennifer's round blue eyes filling with tears when I clumsily told her right before health class that my mother said I couldn't be her friend. I didn't really know how to communicate the news to her, and I am quite confident I did it badly. She asked why, and I told her about the note, the cussing. Like a true friend fighting for her sidekick, she even offered to talk to my parents and dissuade them. We stayed casual friends, but we were no longer best friends. She eventually moved away, and I never saw her again. But back then I was learning about breaking friendships for what was deemed the necessary good, setting standards, and trying desperately to keep them in spite of the cost.

We all have our own bill of rights for friendship, don't we? Though largely unwritten, we have an internal dialogue of what is expected, acceptable, or unacceptable in our relationships.

What are the requirements you set for friendships? Is it time, is it loyalty, is it being there—I mean being really *there*, deep in the mire alongside you, being present to celebrate successes and to mourn disappointments and devastations? Is it hospitality? Is it service? Is it knowing the right words to make you feel better? Is it being with you to mark life's inescapable milestones: births and birthdays, deaths and funerals, illnesses and remissions?

Do we actually know what our own bill of rights requires? Expectations are often sneaky that way. We can be oblivious to them until they go unmet, and then suddenly they seem so obvious they obstruct our vision of anything else. If we haven't identified our requirements, we certainly can't communicate them. Would a bill of rights force each of us to explore our own expectations before they are returned to us unmet and their emptiness swallows us whole?

What do we expect from our friends, and what happens when they don't deliver on those expectations? Margaret Mitchell, the author of *Gone with the Wind,* said, "Life does not have an obligation to give you what you expect."[4] But do our friends? Do we obligate our friends to meet our expectations? And if they are unable to do so, should we extricate ourselves from the friendship?

Well, maybe. But I think collectively we probably run the gamut from discarding friendships too quickly to the other end of the spectrum, where we allow ourselves to be doormats or punching bags in the name of friendship. And really, how do we measure the distance between sacrifice, service, and slavery? Do we serve out of fear or kindness, offer acceptance out of guilt or grace?

The large number of women who are depleted emotionally, physically, and spiritually suggests that much of the time we are unclear about how much to give and whether it's okay to receive as well. The Christian call to service, love, and laying down one's life for our friends adds a layer of guilt to the confusion, as we practically cringe at even saying the word "me" or "I."

We're not particularly comfortable with the idea of rights in the context of relationships. It sounds selfish and demanding. After all, aren't we supposed to die to self? Where is the how-to book telling us when to renew our commitment to a friendship and when the friendship is becoming destructive to one of us? Truthfully, I don't think we know how to do this well. And this land mine has largely remained buried.

I'm not sure how old I was, but sometime in the 1980s, I remember catching *Oprah* one afternoon after school. That particular day Oprah gave women permission to do something that, along with other female voices of influence, spawned a movement. She told women it was okay to say words like *no* and *I.* As worn-out woman after woman confessed to walking a dangerous ledge of exhaustion, depleted internal resources, and emotional barrenness all in the name of selflessness, Oprah gave women everywhere permission to say, "Enough."

Others quickly jumped on the bandwagon, and with such force pushing against it, the pendulum swung far to the other side, as is often the way of movements. Selflessness became almost synonymous with weakness, and nurturance faced extinction. Eventually there was a bandwagon against that too, and we rode it until we arrived somewhere in the middle. I'm not quite sure where the evangelical church has landed, though. When I was writing my book *Transparent,* I interviewed about twenty women, and a number of them spoke candidly about a lifetime of giving and enabling others without caring for themselves, either spiritually or emotionally. The effects of this neglect had been grave for several of them, on both their physical bodies and their families.

I think we are more comfortable maintaining a bill of rights in regard to careers and secular work, but in the name of sacred work, we run the race right into the ground while people stand on the sidelines and cheer us on in our self-destructing burnout in the name of God.

And in much the same way, in the name of selflessness, love, and service, we empower destructive behaviors, unintentionally abetting the weaknesses of others, even enduring their mistreatment of us in our friendships, needing—wanting—to be their greatest friend, the selfless woman. In a word, *perfect*. And with all honesty and with noble intentions set aside for a moment, it hurts us to hurt someone else and to experience the loss of a broken friendship.

I still smart when I think back to the eighth grade and breaking my friendship in obedience to my parents. So often the decision to choose self over destructive patterns in a friendship is accompanied with a hearty helping of guilt—and no substitutions. Then in order to digest our decision and live with it, we are often forced to demonize the friend to both others and ourselves, as though we need blame to fill the space that our broken friendship has created. Why can't we let the space just be? Why is the space like a quiet moment in a conversation we feel an obligation to fill? Why are we so uncomfortable with space?

Yet there are times in a friendship when we must grant ourselves—and our friend—the space we need to step to the side and then forward. Sometimes that space will be permanent. To actually speak directly of a parting of the relationship with her takes more courage than simply letting it drift away with the ebb of time and flow of busyness. Yet, if we intend the severance for her good as well, we must summon that courage.

Where do we find the resources we need to take this step and live with it? Because surely courage of conviction is required not only to make the decision to end a relationship but also to remain resolute in our commitment to this difficult decision. Where do we begin to find the courage? It begins, I believe, with friendship with self.

FOURTEEN

A Branch of Friendship

She wrote my dad a letter, describing her feelings of isolation in her faith. The only person of faith within her immediate atheistic family, she made her commitment after being invited to church by a friend from school. Alone, she struggles in her growth, working through difficult questions without immediate answers. In her letter she asked if my dad would call her. He did, and they spoke at length about matters of faith, questions on her mind, her struggle of being alone in her faith among those who mean the most to her.

After conversing for some time, my dad asked her if she had any more questions. "Just one," she said. "Can you tell me why I don't like so many people?" It was a serious question, a question so adult in its search for an intelligent answer, yet so childlike in its unflinching honesty. I championed her boldness in putting forth the question and understood her feeling, though I'd never before put it into words.

There are certainly times when I feel like I don't like a lot of people. Or at least, I feel let down by them. There was a period when my thoughts constantly entertained disappointments about this person and then another person, mostly having to do with my feeling personally let down because they didn't respond to things the way I anticipated or behave toward me the way I wanted. I had begun an unconscious exercise of too often rattling off a list of disappointments and letdowns. Eventually I became irritated at my own internal dialogue of self-pity. My complaining seemed annoyingly near constant.

One day it occurred to me to wonder, *If I feel continuously let down by so many friendships in my life, is there another problem here?* The frequency was what drew my attention. I began to wonder if the problem might be me and my expectations. It at least warranted exploration, and so I retreated to my head, taking up residence there for the day, examining these thoughts, tracing through my feelings.

I realized that perhaps I was looking in the wrong place for many of the things I wasn't finding. Was I looking to my friends to keep me from feelings of loneliness? Was I asking them to be responsible for my opinion of myself, to give worth to my journey—where I'd been and what I'd learned? Was I looking to them to provide confidence in what I already knew to be true of my faith, my walk with God? Was I asking them to make up for past relationships that had wronged me? Was I asking them to help me accept my body, my gifts, my talents?

Perhaps I was asking my friends for something they were never supposed to give to me. Perhaps I needed to look elsewhere for the answer to these needs. Could it be that some of what I was searching for could only be found buried deep within myself—and in a friendship with myself? If so, to realize these needs I would have to learn to cultivate that friendship with self.

Why does friendship with self seem like an uncomfortable relationship to discuss? The truth is we have known ourselves longer than we have known any other human being. So why does friendship with ourselves seem so unpracticed? Are we prone to worry about those who spend too much time alone? Do we sometimes even loathe being alone with ourselves, choosing solitude only as a final recourse to alleviate our frustration with people? Is self the last-resort friend, when nothing better has come along?

In many ways, for all our familiarity with friendship, being our own friend is the aspect we least understand. What does it mean exactly? Is this merely self-help, feel-good fluff? What does a friendship with self look like? The giving of time, acceptance, forgiveness, patience, respect—these are characteristics of our friendships with others. Can they be given to ourselves as well? As I have explored the idea, I have indeed found that friendship with self requires all of these qualities. But how do we do this?

The first step is giving time—setting aside time for your thoughts, time to meditate, time to simply be. Our lives as we know them rarely give us the gift of solitude, so we must be intentional in carving out that time. Bear in mind that friendship with self does not eliminate God; rather, it allows a greater friendship with God. Learning to have a friendship with self requires spending time in solitude with your own thoughts and with God. Whether through prayer, reading the Word, inhabiting nature, or merely stillness, friendship with God gives sustenance to our very souls.

We delight in feeling known. A friendship with self means that, inasmuch as we know our friends, we know ourselves too. In the way we sense that a friend is not being entirely honest with us, we know too when we are not being honest with ourselves. In friendship with self we are able to recognize our motives, our excuses, and our justifications for what we think, do, and say for what they truly are.

We are all fully aware, often painfully aware, of the humanity of others, and in times of honesty and self-awareness, we see our own humanity as well. In friendship with self we learn to accept where we are. We cease the constant inner dialogue of judgment. And we allow patience to creep into our souls.

God will take a lifetime to accomplish what he has for us. Patience with your journey and ownership of it—knowing that it is *your* journey—is friendship with self. Only through time spent alone and with God can we be comfortable in our aloneness and comforted by God's acceptance and love. This means looking into the mirror reflected back by God, that is, seeing our humanity, our sinful nature, but also the grace afforded to us, the forgiveness, and the worth.

We know we have worth because we are created in the image of God. We know God loves each one of us. We are worth so much that we were worth dying for. Teresa of Avila, a spiritual reformer who, like many of her predecessors, spent time in the solitude of convent living, wrote to those who studied under her, "Let us imagine that within us is an extremely rich palace, built entirely of gold and precious stones.... Within us lies something incomparably more precious than what we see outside ourselves."[1] We recognize this value in ourselves only as we see the image of God in us and then in others.

As we respect our friends, we also learn to respect ourselves. When we respect our friends, we respect their personhood as well as their gifts and talents from which we so often benefit. We take care to treat our friends kindly, to care for their souls rather than bring hurt. Out of respect we refuse to cross certain lines where our friends are concerned. We are careful not to offend or violate boundaries, and we would not want to do a friend physical harm. Yet often we trespass against ourselves in ways we would never trespass against another or even allow someone else to do against us. In friendship with self we learn to bring the same respect to ourselves. Like the Bill of Rights for Friends, there are lines we will not cross within ourselves or let others cross.

Friendship with self does not eliminate community or the need for it. Nor is it a friendship you practice only when you have no other friends. Rather friendships with ourselves allow us to connect and participate in community in a richer and fuller way. Some of the women who belonged to the consciousness-raising groups of the late sixties and early seventies said of the community many years later, "The collective enables the personal."[2] It was the collective journey in community that made possible individual awareness of the work to be done in each person's life. The need for friendship with self is necessary even in community. A woman at an AA meeting noted wisely her own personal discovery: "If I don't accept myself, then I can't accept others." If we believe God wants us to love others, then for the same reasons and out of the same faith, we must love ourselves too.

Still, the idea of friendship with self perhaps sits uncomfortably with us as we are also confronted with our need for forgiveness, for redemption, and our call to love and serve others. Much in the same way that a friendship with another does not elevate her to a position of perfection, accepting ourselves does not preclude needing forgiveness from God and from others when we have wronged them or intentionally seeking that forgiveness. And contrary to loving only self, friendship of self enables us to love others.

When we behave toward ourselves in a way that is unloving, when we are judgmental and disparaging of our individuality, we are not being good friends. Would you want to be friends with someone who told you that you are unlovable, unattractive, undesirable, or unintelligent? We would say assuredly that such a person is a friend to release, and yet we speak these messages within ourselves.

Edith Stein discusses the importance of realizing the "concrete wholeness of an individual," a combination of "authentic humanity and womanhood with an unspoiled individuality."[3] The wisdom of her expressed ideas lies, I believe, in the aspect of healthy combination. To be awakened to "authentic humanity" is to know our own flaws, our tendencies, and our vast imperfections, and yet "unspoiled individuality" speaks to the beauty and value of the individual who, not in spite of but along with her humanity, is a stunning creation, one fashioned in the image of God. How can she be anything but unspoiled then?

Stein goes on to say, "But especially needed are faith in one's own being and courage regarding it, as well as faith in one's individual calling to definite personal activities and a ready willingness to follow this call."[4] To be in relationship with self, to be a friend to ourselves requires this faith and this courage. It is not arrogance nor a declaration of self-sufficiency, without need of God or others; it is an acknowledgment of the innate value placed within ourselves and honors the value that others then speak into our lives through their friendship. If we believe God has called each of us to a purpose, then within our individuality God has placed the tools to follow our calling.

By rooting ourselves to that which God calls us, we yield the fruit he has given us in due time. And this fruit is seen in how we love others. So perhaps the humanity of our jealousy of others, our competitive nature as women, and our judgment of others reveals our unrealized acceptance of ourselves. "The vocation of every Christian," says Stein, "is to awaken and further the life of grace in souls wherever the possibility exists. But woman assumes this vocation in a special way, thanks to her special relationship to the Lord who has destined her for it."[5]

By nurturing a friendship with self, we develop a completeness in our humanity as God has created us, and in this strength we are able to give to others more fully, more completely. And it is enough. To be there in sorrow and in joy, to know what you can and cannot give, and to give what you can freely.

Sometimes I imagine myself to be a tree. For a time I imagined myself to be any old tree, and then I decided to choose one particular kind to be, thinking it might help in my visualization. And so I chose a willow tree, simply because willows are my favorite. I think willows are strong yet graceful. Their long limbs spread far, offering shade and beauty, even privacy as their slender branches hang so low they nearly drag along the earth's floor. Most remarkable perhaps are the roots of the willow, their size, their resiliency, and their tenacity.

Often willow trees are planted along the edge of a stream or river where their roots can protect the bank from the erosion of the water. Willows take root easily and quickly. Even a fallen limb can take root and grow. And there's an element of sadness to willow trees that I feel at ease with. I imagine a tree like the fantastical tree in "Pictor's Metamorphoses," which is the story of a man who, in a search for happiness in paradise, was transformed into a tree, "lonely and sad, and yet beautiful, touching, and noble in its mute sorrow."[6]

When I'm imagining I am a willow tree, I stand tall, bringing one foot to the top of my opposite leg and placing that foot flat against the inside of my thigh. Standing ever so still, I balance on my standing leg. When my leg is steady, I slowly bring my arms above my head, eventually spreading them wide above me. And there I stand, rooted by my foot planted to the floor below me. I feel where my foot connects to the floor, and then as I sink lower, I feel the distinction no more. As I stand still, my arms raised, I feel elongated, tall and strong. I feel the strength in my "trunk," my thighs and hips, as they steady me, allowing me to stand strong. I feel the energy racing through my quadriceps, and I tighten those muscles to further support my weight. I stay in that position until my muscles tremble and I can no longer hold it. Then I switch legs and do the same thing, balancing on the other foot.

There is something life giving about imagining myself as another part of God's creation, solitary yet filled with the presence and strength of God. I picture myself planted to the earth, drawing nutrients so I can have life, grow, and flourish. I chose a tree in part because nature has always connected me to God. Whether in its power, breathtaking beauty, or simplicity, nature always evokes a spiritual response from my soul. And I chose a tree because since I was a little girl, I've identified with trees in a particular way, though I'm not sure why.

My grandmother used to exclaim over and over at an exquisite sunset, finding all of them exquisite, and of course they are. One particular dusk when I was very young, the sky was streaked with spectacular washes of purple, pink, and orange. As we took in its glow, my grandmother fervently declared that the sky was her favorite aspect of God's creation. I quietly replied that trees were mine.

Perhaps it's that often trees are forgotten. Their beauty seems quieter than the grandeur of a sunset or the power of foamy waves that command our awe and respect. Many of us ignore trees, taking from them what we want—fruit, shade, or lumber—and then forget all about them. Mostly we don't think much about trees until fall, when, in many parts of the country, they seem to suddenly tire of being forgotten, of seeing all the attention directed elsewhere. They erupt in a performance much like a child who tires of playing second fiddle to a more talented or charismatic sibling. Suddenly trees rival the colorful symphony played by the sun most evenings. I remember one year driving up the winding roads to the mountains the week before Thanksgiving. I took a turn that gave me a panoramic view of the mountains blanketed by a kaleidoscope of color. Deep in hues of red, rust, and gold, the beauty of the view invited tears to my eyes.

Whatever the reason or origin, no matter the season, I developed a feeling of connection to the image of the tree and even assumed it was an image unique to my own thoughts. I discovered, though, that literature, legends, and psychology are rife with the symbolism and archetypes of trees. The willow tree, for example, is a frequently seen image in Eastern literature. The Bible, too, uses trees as symbols. The very first psalm tells us,

> Blessed is the man
>> who does not walk in the counsel of the wicked
> or stand in the way of sinners
>> or sit in the seat of mockers.

But his delight is in the law of the LORD,
    and on his law he meditates day and night.
He is like a tree planted by streams of water,
    which yields its fruit in season
and whose leaf does not wither.[7]

I think of the tree as a picture of friendship too. Like the tree, friendship has seasons of life and death, the yielding of fruit or flowers that is life giving to others. In friendship there is a deep and abiding root structure and long, graceful arms that reach far, having much to give. To sustain life, trees and friendships require nutrients from another source. And when cut down a lone branch will take root once more and begin again.

And so as I stretch my body in this exercise of the tree, I nurture my soul and mind in prayerful solitude. It is my meditation and part of my practice of friendship with myself. Only then do I find the strength for friendship outside myself. Only then can I stretch my arms wide in giving and receiving. Only then is friendship complete.

Discussion Guide

THE DEFINITIONS

1. Which qualities do you most appreciate in a friend? Are these qualities present in your current friendships?
2. How would you define a friend?
3. In what ways do your friendships enrich your life? In what ways do you enrich the lives of your friends?

THE CONNECTION

4. The laotong women of China shared a secret language. Do you and your friends share a language understood by only your close-knit group? In what way does that language bond you with your friends?
5. Do you feel free to be your genuine self with your friends? Or do you feel the need to put on a pretense to be accepted? What makes you feel safe to just be yourself?
6. Sarah states that women's friendships are characterized by conflict, jealousy, competitiveness, betrayal, and disappointment but that they ultimately demonstrate loyalty, availability, kindred spirits,

forgiveness, and fierce strength. In which ways do these qualities mirror your experience? Does the scale balance between these opposite characteristics?

7. Do you place demands on your friends? What do they demand of you?

8. How do your friendships meet your need for connection? for community? What roles do you play to achieve that sense of connection? Are you the rescuer? the nurturer? the needy one? Or do these roles shift from time to time?

The Challenges, Wounds, and Trickiness

9. Do you ever experience jealousy and competitiveness in your friendships? How do they manifest themselves? How do they get resolved? What toll do they take on the relationships?

10. Have you ever found yourself the target of gossiping friends? How did that make you feel? What did you do about it? How did it impact the future of those friendships?

11. Have you ever felt betrayed by a close friend? How did that impact your relationship? Was reconciliation possible? What was the outcome?

12. Have you ever had to confront a friend with a difficult truth? How did you approach that conversation? What was your friend's reaction?

13. Has betrayal or misconduct ever fractured one of your friendships? Was it difficult to make the decision to either mend or end the relationship? What was the deciding factor?

14. Loving a friend when all is well is often easier than forgiving her and renewing the covenant of friendship after a betrayal or a confrontation. What's helped you restore a fractured relationship? Did it require a process of time and commitment to forgive? What helped you reach total forgiveness?

15. Where do you draw the line between renewing your commitment to a difficult friendship and deciding it has become destructive and needs to end? If you've chosen to end a friendship, how did you reach your ultimate decision? Do you experience guilt over your decision?

16. Do you have a mental list of disappointments with friends that has left you wondering about their commitment to you? What are three things you expect your friends to do for you? List them, then ask yourself if these are realistic expectations. Are these three things something they are able to give you?

THE SEASONS AND EBB AND FLOW

17. Sarah asks, "Is there an age of friendship? Is there a time when our friendships are richer, deeper, even

more in number?" How have your friendships changed? Do you still give the same priority to friendships the way you used to? What changed? When did it change, and why?

18. Anamchara, the ministry of soul friendships, represented a vital part of Celtic spirituality. Have you been blessed with a soul friend? In what ways has that friend ministered to you? What makes that friendship special?

19. Do your deepest, most satisfying friendships sometimes need a hiatus, a space, leaving you feeling uncertain about your relationship? When your expectations and needs for connection are not met, how do you respond? How do you gather confidence to accept your friend, even when she seems to withdraw?

20. Most of us experience a friendship that lasts for a season and then is gone. Think about a time when this has happened for you. Was the relationship discontinued for geographical reasons, a major life change, or some other reason? Were you able to grieve it and then let it go, or do you still miss that connection?

THE ESSENCE

21. Has a close friend held up a mirror to you, allowing you to see something about yourself that you had

previously not seen? Did this new image of yourself cut like a shard of glass or reveal an unknown aspect of your beauty? Did it cause you to take a deeper look at the reflection of yourself?

22.   Is there a particular friend who opens your eyes to the beauties of life, to the wonder of creation, to the goodness of God's presence on the earth? What unique gifts does this friend bring that nurture your soul? What do you learn from her?

23.   Are you involved in a group or community of people that enhances your individual friendships? Did you find this group at church? in your local community? through a particular shared interest or passion? How does this group enrich your individual friendships?

24.   When more than two friends gather together, jealousy, competition, and backbiting seem to flourish. Have you seen this occur within your group of friends? What seems to create this dynamic? How does it play out in your group of friends? Does a sense of loyalty and camaraderie prevail despite the competitiveness?

25.   What is your personal bill of rights for friendship? What do you want and need in a friend? What are your rights and responsibilities? What are her rights and responsibilities?

26. How do you define a healthy friendship with yourself? What is your bill of rights for a friendship with yourself? Do you give yourself time, acceptance, care, forgiveness, grace, patience, and respect? If so, in what ways do you give these gifts to yourself?

Acknowledgments

Once more, I am enormously grateful to Jeannette Thomason, my editor. I am so grateful to her for trusting me with this project, and I cannot say enough what a gift it is not only to work with her but to learn from her. I also want to thank Laura Barker for her hard work and the graceful way she guided it all to completion.

I am thankful too, to Tina Jacobson, my agent, for her steadfast support and most of all for her friendship. I am deeply grateful to Alan Gary for his unwavering support, his countless good ideas and sources, and his inspiration.

And I am filled with gratitude to Naomi for staying up all night to read the manuscript just to give me feedback and for believing in me, and to Jill, Bridget, and Naomi once more for all the conversations and support that inspired so much.

And to all who steadily cheered me on and were patient with me too as I struggled through this endeavor—my mom and dad, my brother, Nate, my friends Joyce and Nelson—I am deeply appreciative.

Notes

CHAPTER 1

1. Cicero, *De Amicitia,* quoted in *A Friendship Book* (New York: MJF Books, 2005), 5.

2. Lisa See, *Snow Flower and the Secret Fan* (New York: Random House, 2005).

3. Aristotle, quoted in Diogenes Laertius, *Lives of Eminent Philosophers,* trans. R. D. Hicks, "Aristotle," bk. 5, sct. 20 (London: William Heinemann, 1925); Ralph Waldo Emerson, "Friendship," in *Essays,* First Series (1841), quoted in *The Columbia World of Quotations* (New York: Columbia University Press, 1996).

4. F. W. Boreham, "Befriending One's Fears," *All the Blessings of Life* (Eureka, CA: John Broadbanks, 2007).

5. L. M. Montgomery, *Anne of Green Gables* (New York: Bantam Books, 1976), 58–59.

6. C. S. Lewis, *The Four Loves,* in *The Inspirational Writings of C. S. Lewis* (New York: Inspirational, 1994), 244.

7. Lewis, *The Four Loves,* 261.

CHAPTER 2

1. Louann Brizendine, *The Female Brain* (New York: Broadway Books, 2006), 29.

2. Louisa May Alcott, *Little Women* (Ann Arbor: Ann Arbor Media, 2006), 49.

3. Susan Hazen-Hammond, "First Woman and the People," in *Spider Woman's Web* (New York: Berkley Publishing, 1999), 87–93.

4. Carol Gilligan, *In a Different Voice* (Cambridge: Harvard University Press, 1982, 1993), 35.

5. Lia Macko and Kerry Rubin, *Midlife Crisis at 30* (Emmaus, PA: Rodale, 2004), 63–64.

6. Carol Lee Flinders, *At the Root of This Longing* (San Francisco: HarperCollins, 1999), 112–13.

7. Brizendine, *The Female Brain,* 21, 29.

8. Gilligan, *In a Different Voice,* 43.

9. Macko and Rubin, *Midlife Crisis at 30,* 66.

10. Macko and Rubin, *Midlife Crisis at 30,* 66.

11. Macko and Rubin, *Midlife Crisis at 30,* 68.

CHAPTER 3

1. Linda Carroll, "Psst! Gossip May Be Good for You," MSNBC.com—Mental Health, July 18, 2007, www.msnbc.msn.com/id/19748142/wid/11915773 ?GT1=10212.

2. Rosalind Wiseman, *Queen Bees and Wannabes* (New York: Three Rivers, 2002), 122.

3. Wiseman, *Queen Bees,* 122.

4. Carroll, "Psst! Gossip May Be Good for You."

5. Wiseman, *Queen Bees,* 121.

6. Carol Lee Flinders, *At the Root of This Longing* (San Francisco: HarperCollins, 1999), 114.

CHAPTER 4

1. Dietrich Bonhoeffer, *Dietrich Bonhoeffer's Christmas Sermons,* ed. and trans. Edwin Robertson (Grand Rapids: Zondervan, 2005), 67.

CHAPTER 5

1. John 15:13.

2. Christopher Bamford, "The Joy of Two," *Parabola* 29, no. 4 (November 2004): 13.

CHAPTER 6

1. C. S. Lewis, *The Four Loves,* in *The Inspirational Writings of C. S. Lewis* (New York: Inspirational, 1994), 244.

2. Naomi Schaefer Riley, "The Young and the Restless: Why Infidelity Is Rising Among 20-Somethings," *Wall Street Journal,* November 27, 2008, http://online.wsj.com/article/SB122782458360062499.html.

3. Lewis, *The Four Loves,* 254.

4. Lewis, *The Four Loves,* 256.

CHAPTER 7

1. Rosalind Wiseman, *Queen Bees and Wannabes* (New York: Three Rivers, 2002), 162.
2. Edward Sellner, *The Celtic Soul Friend* (Notre Dame, IN: Ave Maria, 2002), 14.
3. Sellner, *The Celtic Soul Friend,* 79.
4. Henri Nouwen, *Out of Solitude* (Notre Dame, IN: Ave Maria, 1974, 2004), 38.

CHAPTER 8

1. John O'Donohue, *Eternal Echoes* (New York: Harper-Collins, 1999), 55.
2. O'Donohue, *Eternal Echoes,* 56.
3. 2 Samuel 12:1–14.
4. Louann Brizendine, *The Female Brain* (New York: Broadway Books, 2006), 118.
5. Rumi, from *The Essential Rumi,* expanded edition (San Francisco: HarperCollins, 2004), 141–42.
6. O'Donohue, *Eternal Echoes,* 58.

CHAPTER 9

1. Ruth 1–3.

CHAPTER 10

1. Catharine Fournier, "Saint Clare of Assisi," Domestic-Church.com, Saint Profile: "St. Clare

of Assisi" http://domestic-church.com/
CONTENT.DCC/19980701/SAINTS/
ST_CLARE.htm.

2. Anita Shreve, *Women Together, Women Alone*
(New York: Viking, 1989), 12.

3. Shreve, *Women Together, Women Alone.*

4. Carol Lee Flinders, *At the Root of This Longing*
(San Francisco: HarperCollins, 1999), 51–52.

5. Anne Morrow Lindbergh, *Gift from the Sea* (New
York: Pantheon, 1997), 30.

CHAPTER 11

1. Virginia Woolf, *The Waves* (Orlando: Harcourt,
1931), 90.

2. Carol Gilligan, *In a Different Voice* (Cambridge:
Harvard University Press, 1982, 1993), 42–43.

CHAPTER 12

1. W. B. Yeats, "To the Rose upon the Rood of Time,"
The Rose, stanza 2, lines 1–2.

2. Anne Morrow Lindbergh, *Gift from the Sea* (New
York: Pantheon, 1997), 109.

CHAPTER 13

1. Henry Wadsworth Longfellow, "The Fire of Drift-
wood," stanzas 1–5.

2. George Eliot, *Daniel Deronda* (Chicago: Belford, Clarke, 1886), 344.

3. Rosalind Wiseman, *Queen Bees and Wannabes* (New York: Three Rivers, 2002), 173.

4. Margaret Mitchell, quoted in Lia Macko and Kerry Rubin, *Midlife Crisis at 30* (Emmaus, PA: Rodale, 2004), 27.

CHAPTER 14

1. Teresa of Avila, *Way of Perfection,* quoted in Carol Lee Flinders, *At the Root of This Longing* (San Francisco: HarperCollins, 1999), 166–67.

2. Anita Shreve, *Women Together, Women Alone* (New York: Viking, 1989), 197.

3. Edith Stein, *Essays on Woman,* trans. Freda Mary Oben (Washington, DC: ICS, 1996), 202.

4. Stein, *Essays on Woman,* 202.

5. Stein, *Essays on Woman,* 239.

6. Hermann Hesse, "Pictor's Metamorphoses," in *Pictor's Metamorphoses and Other Fantasies* (New York: Noonday, 1981), 119.

7. Psalm 1:1–3.

About the Author

Sarah Zacharias Davis is the vice president of marketing and development for Ravi Zacharias International Ministries, having joined the ministry after working in strategic marketing for CNN. She graduated from Covenant College with a degree in education and now lives in Atlanta, Georgia. She is the daughter of best-selling author Ravi Zacharias and the author of two books, *Confessions from an Honest Wife* and *Transparent: Getting Honest About Who We Are and Who We Want to Be.*